WINDOWS

WINDOWS
EDL GO Series Book 2

EDITORS

Daniel J. Domoff
Estelle Kleinman

COMPREHENSION QUESTIONS AND SHORT PIECES BY

Edith Goldstein

ILLUSTRATOR

Anthony D'Adamo

Art Director/Designer – Ronald Wickham

Cover design by Roger M. Wolters

*Cover photography courtesy
of Champion Papers,
IMAGINATION XII–San Francisco*

ISBN 1-55855-662-1

CONTENTS

BAD JOE AND SAM DASHER

**In just one day,
everything seems to backfire
on Bad Joe.**

Back about 80 years ago, a lot of people walked around with guns here in Yuko City. They didn't need them much. The country around here was mostly quiet by then. But, as I said, some people liked to keep those guns on. Maybe they didn't feel safe without them. Who knows?

Now, there was a man around here named Bad Joe. And let me tell you, he was bad! He loved to pick fights. He had big, heavy fists. One blow from his fist could put you out cold! Most people stayed away from Bad Joe and his gang.

One day Bad Joe was sitting in Ned's Place with some of his gang. People used to go to Ned's Place to eat, drink, play checkers, and play cards. Joe was playing cards. He had lost some money, and he

1

wasn't very happy about it. No, he wasn't very happy about it at all. You could just tell that Bad Joe was looking for a fight.

So after some time, Sam Dasher came into Ned's Place. Sam was new in Yuko City. He worked in the bank. He was young and well dressed. I don't think he'd ever been inside of Ned's Place before.

Bad Joe saw Sam come in. Now, Joe must have thought right away that he could win some of his money back. So Joe called out, "You! Come on over here and sit down! Come on over!"

Sam walked over to Joe's table and sat down. He took off his gloves. "My name is Sam Dasher," he said. "I'm new here."

"My name," said Bad Joe, "is Joe. Nothing more. Just Joe. And these men are my friends. Now that we've said who we are, let's play cards."

"All right," said Sam.

They played draw poker. Bad Joe was winning at first, but then he started getting some bad cards. Sam Dasher started winning Joe's money. Joe's face was getting hot. People started watching the game. Things got quiet. You could just tell that Joe was going to blow up.

Bad Joe was giving out the cards.

"How many cards do you want?" he asked Sam.

"Two," said Sam. He had three fives in his hand. He turned in two cards and got two new ones.

"And I want two cards too," said Joe.

The betting was heavy. A lot of money was on the table. Joe's friends dropped out. Just Bad Joe and

Sam were left.

"What have you got?" said Joe.

Sam put his cards face up on the table. "Four fives!" he said.

"I win!" said Bad Joe. "I have four tens!" He put his cards on the table too, and then started to take the money.

"Wait!" said Sam. "You can't have four tens! I had a ten before I asked for cards. You can't have four tens!"

Bad Joe gave him a hard, hard look.

"Are you saying that I cheated?"

"Yes!" said Sam.

The room was quiet. No one said a word. Everyone looked on, waiting.

"I'll make you eat dirt for that!" said Bad Joe. "No one calls me a cheater. Get your gun and come out to the street!"

Sam knew by then that he was in a lot of trouble. So he said to Joe, "Well, maybe I was wrong. Why don't we forget it? You win."

"Forget nothing!" Bad Joe's eyes were dark. "Get a gun or I'll shoot you right here!"

Sam could hardly talk. "But I don't have a gun," he said.

"Here's a gun," someone said. That was a good thing about Yuko City! Someone was always ready to help out!

Sam had to take that gun, and somehow he got out into the street. Bad Joe came after him, and so did everyone in the room.

Bad Joe walked down the street a ways. When he got to the warehouse, he turned to face Sam. If Sam didn't do some trick or something, he was going to get shot, right then and there!

"Draw!" said Joe.

Sam did try to draw his gun. But Bad Joe was much faster. Joe fired! Sam didn't even get his gun out!

But nothing happened to Sam! Everyone looked at Bad Joe. Something was wrong with Joe's gun! All it did was blow up in his hand! Bad Joe's right hand would never be right again!

After that, no one in Yuko City walked around with a gun anymore. Sam Dasher stayed out of Ned's Place from then on. And Bad Joe? No one called him "Bad Joe" anymore. Everyone called him "Lefty." And he never cheated at cards again.

Old Silver, Old Gold

Is there a fast and easy way to make money? Bill and Alice find it long, hard work.

The sea was quiet. Too quiet. I was sitting in the boat, waiting for Bill to come up from under the water. He'd been down on the sea floor for nearly an hour, and I was getting a little worried.

But I was always a little worried in those days. Bill and I were looking for a ship that had gone down in a storm about 400 years ago. An old story said that the ship had had gold and silver on board. Whoever could find it would make a million dollars! Anyway, that's what we hoped.

We knew that the ship had gone down in these waters, only about ten miles from shore. So the gold and silver had to be somewhere nearby! But we knew too that the gold and silver could have been covered by many feet of sand. It was going to be some job to find it.

I looked over the side of the boat. There was no sign of Bill. I knew he couldn't stay down much longer. I never liked it when he went down without me. Anything can happen under water. But two people can always watch out for one another.

At last I saw something move. Yes—it was Bill, coming back up. He got to the boat, and I helped him get in.

"Don't ever do that again!" I said. "You were down a long time."

"Never mind!" he said. "Alice, look at this!"

Bill had two pieces of old gold money in his hand.

"Is there more?" I asked.

"I can't tell. There may be a lot more under the sand. We'll have to dig."

"Did you see the ship?"

"No. But I did see some old pieces of wood. They lay just about ten feet from where I picked up the gold."

"Do you think the wood was from the ship?" I asked.

"Could be. But I wouldn't bet on it."

I should say that when a ship goes down in a storm, it takes some time to go under. For a time it stays on the water and moves about in the storm. It may move as far as a mile before it goes down at last. As the ship moves, things fall out of it little by little, things like gold and silver. Most of the gold and silver would have landed in one place. But some could have landed in other places. So Bill didn't know if he had come across most of it or just a bit of it.

Bill and I got ready to go down together.

Many brave people have died looking for gold under water. I didn't want to be one of them. So we checked everything two times before going down. When everything was right, down we went. Even so, I didn't like leaving our boat with no one in it. It's not a smart thing to do. But that's the way it had to be, because there were only two of us.

Digging in the sand on the sea floor is a hard and dirty job. The water gets cloudy with dirt. You can see for only about five feet. You can look and look and see nothing. And that's what we got for all our trouble. Nothing.

When we came back up, we knew right away that we had more trouble. Another boat was nearby, with about 15 men and women on it. They were looking for the gold too.

Bill was mad. "How did they know that we were looking for the ship here? We never aid a word to anyone!"

"When it comes to gold and silver," I said, "word gets around. Anyway, we know there's nothing here. Let's move."

We moved. And we moved again. Little by little, we started to find some silver and gold. Now we could go down only one at a time. One of us had to stay on the boat to watch our gold and silver.

We did this for a week, going from one place to another. Here and there, we came across some of the money. But we failed to find the place where most of it had gone down. Maybe we had gone past it. There was no way of telling.

Bill and I began to run out of gas and food. We had to get back to land. We knew we could get good money for the gold and silver we had. But we were sad that we couldn't find the rest of it.

The other boat? They didn't find anything. So the rest of the gold and silver is down there to this day. Bill and I will look for it again some day. We'll find it.

The Catch of Time

Who is to say what books you may or may not read? The people of Stanton find that this is not an easy question to answer.

The trouble began in the fall and lasted for most of the school year. Before fall, Stanton had been a quiet city. But after the trouble, Stanton was changed.

Marla was in her last year of school. She was walking home one day with a book in her hand.

"How are you, Marla?" It was Mr. Sitwell, who lived next door. "How's school?" Mr. Sitwell always asked a lot of questions.

"It's OK," Marla answered. "School is school."

"What's that book you're reading?" asked Mr. Sitwell.

"Something called *The Catch of Time*. I'm reading it for one of my courses at school."

Mr. Sitwell's eyes bugged open. "You're reading *The Catch of Time*? Don't you know that's a dirty book?"

"No," said Marla. "I didn't know that. There's nothing in it so far that's dirty."

Mr. Sitwell was shaking. "Well, it *is* a dirty book," he said. "They shouldn't give you that book in school! No one should read it!"

And that's how the trouble began.

Mr. Sitwell called a meeting of some of his friends. They mailed letters to the Stanton school board and to the Stanton newspapers. All the letters said, "Get rid of *The Catch of Time*. It is poisoning our children's minds."

The story came out in the newspapers the next day. It said, "Some people in Stanton don't like the lessons our children are learning in school. These people want to take *The Catch of Time* out of the Stanton schools. They say it's a dirty book."

Marla put down *The Catch of Time*. She was done reading it. Then she went to talk to her teacher. "I feel so bad," Marla said. "I was the one who told Mr. Sitwell that we were reading *The Catch of Time*."

"Don't feel bad," said Marla's teacher. "Why shouldn't he know what you're reading? You have nothing to hide."

"He says it's a dirty book," Marla said. "I've read it. I don't see what he means. There's the part that talks about a little animal being born. But the book is mostly just a love story. Right?"

"Well," said Marla's teacher, "there's a little more to it than that. But, for the most part, it's just a love story. We'll talk about it in class."

In very little time there was a big fight going on in the city of Stanton. All of the parents took sides, and things got hot.

"When I was in school," said Mr. Sitwell, "we learned how to spell and how to write. That came first. But look at what our children are learning now! How to read a dirty book. That book is poison!"

There were many people on the other side of the fence. They said, "If *The Catch of Time* is poison, then so is milk and fruit! It's a good book, and our children should read it."

Many of the young people of Stanton saw the fight as a big joke. They wanted to know what all the trouble was about. So they all started reading *The Catch of Time,* looking for the dirty parts. But some couldn't find anything that looked dirty. And others couldn't understand what they were reading.

David, a young man in Marla's class, was having a very hard time. His parents didn't want him to read the book. But he had to read it for school. David didn't know what to do. He told the teacher what his trouble was.

The teacher said, "Do your parents tell you what movies you can see?"

David said, "Sometimes yes, sometimes no."

"Well," said the teacher, "I won't tell you that you have to read *The Catch of Time*. You must think that one out by yourself."

"Myself?" said David.

"Yourself," said the teacher.

Marla's hand was up. The teacher called on her.

Marla said, "Some people say it's a dirty book. Other people say it isn't. Who's right?"

The teacher said, "The question is not if it's a dirty book. The question is not if it's a good book or a bad book. The question is, who's going to tell you what you may read? Your parents? Yourself? Or some other people? That's what the question is."

That year, Marla learned what a hard question it was to answer.

Morning Thoughts

It's morning, the start of another new day.
How will it work out? Will things go my way?
How will I play it? This time I'll be smart!
I've got to get out of bed. That's a good
place to start.

GOING BACK TO SCHOOL

Mary dropped out of school and she can't find a job. So she's going back to school. Or is she?

Mary sat drinking her coffee and reading the want ads. She was the only one in the apartment. Her father and brother had left for work hours ago. Not finding any jobs to her liking, Mary put down the paper and looked out the window. It was a hot August morning — not a good time of year to look for a job. She would give up for now and start looking again in the fall.

From the day Mary had dropped out of school, nothing had gone right. That was four years ago. After that, she had found and left job after job. None of them were right for her. Without money, she had to live at home with her father and older brother Morgan. It was all right, but it was not where she wanted to be. At times like these she wished she had a mother to talk to. Her mother had died when Mary was only ten.

Mary had thought about going back to school, but she didn't want to work that hard. That was why she had left school in the first place. No, she would just wait it out. Soon the right job would come along.

Mary got dressed and went out for a walk. She liked to take a walk every morning before it got too hot outdoors. While walking, she saw Mrs. Wilson looking in the window of the dress shop. Mrs. Wilson had five children, but she always had time for Mary. When Mary was young, Mrs. Wilson always gave her change for ice cream. A cleaning woman didn't make enough money to be giving it away to other people's children. But that's just what she did.

"Hi, Mary," Mrs. Wilson called as soon as she saw the younger woman. "What have you been up to?"

"Oh, I've been doing lots of things, Mrs. Wilson."

"Like what?" asked Mrs. Wilson, looking right into Mary's eyes.

All of a sudden, the thought of this woman thinking little of her was too much for Mary. "I've been doing a lot of reading," she said. "I've signed up for night school. That way, I can have a job and go to school at the same time. I've been reading some of the books they teach from so that I can get a head start."

"Good for you! My oldest son went to night school. I have some of his books in my apartment. Drop by and I'll give them to you."

"I will," answered Mary. "But I've got to go now."

"Don't forget to drop by," called Mrs. Wilson as Mary walked away.

"What have I gotten myself into?" Mary asked herself as she walked home. "I'm not going back to school."

The next morning, Morgan was very nice to Mary — too nice. When Mary's father came to get his coffee, he asked her to sit down and drink with him. "You've made me very happy, dear," he told her. "Going back to school is the right thing to do."

"Oh, no!" Mary thought. "Mrs. Wilson must have told them."

As soon as her father and brother were out of the apartment, Mary went out to walk and think. What should she do? What could she say to Mrs. Wilson now to make things right? And what about her father and brother? As she was walking, Mary saw Mrs. Wilson coming up the street. As fast as she could, Mary turned around and walked back to her apartment.

After that, Mary stayed indoors most of the time. She stayed in her room a lot. Her father and brother thought that she was reading books for night school. They never went in to check. If they had, they would have found her looking out the window.

One morning, Mary couldn't stand being indoors any more. She went out for a walk. She walked for a long time, not paying attention to where she was going. Then it happened. She found herself face to face with Mrs. Wilson. She thought about running,

15

but her feet wouldn't move.

"Well, Mary, why haven't you come around to pick up those books?" the older woman asked.

"I just forgot," answered Mary.

Mrs. Wilson gave the young woman a long, hard look. Then she said, "Here's some change for ice cream."

"Mrs. Wilson, I'm not a child any more."

"I believe you are," said Mrs. Wilson. "Only a child would play the games you're playing. It's time to grow up. I know what I'm talking about. I wish I had paid attention when my mother said the same thing to me." With that, she walked away and didn't look back.

Mary ran back to her apartment. Safe in her room, she sat on her bed and cried. She didn't come out for the rest of the day. The next morning, she was afraid to leave her room. What would her father and brother say? Mrs. Wilson must have told them by now. But when she did come out, she found them the same as before.

After her family left for work, Mary went out for her morning walk. All the time she was walking, she was thinking about Mrs. Wilson. Why hadn't the older woman told on her? And what about all the things she had said? Could she be right? Mary walked and thought. She didn't know where she was going. Then she found herself walking right by the night school. She walked on for a time. Then she stopped, turned around, and headed toward the school.

The Believer

**Bonnie finds it hard to tell people what she thinks.
Then she gets help in a strange way.**

"That's my new sales plan for children's clothes," said Ms. Lewis. "How do you like it, Bonnie?" The two women were getting ready to leave the clothing store for the day.

Bonnie thought to herself, "It won't work. It just won't work." Although Bonnie didn't think the plan would work, she wouldn't tell Ms. Lewis. After all, Bonnie worked for Ms. Lewis. "I can't tell the person I work for that her plan won't work," thought Bonnie.

"What do you think of the plan, Bonnie?" asked Ms. Lewis again.

"Go on," Bonnie thought to herself. "Tell her what you think!"

But Bonnie only said, "It will probably work very

well, Ms. Lewis.''

Later, Bonnie was angry with herself. "Why can't I tell people how I feel? What am I so afraid of?"

As Bonnie walked home after work, she saw a sign in a store window. The sign said:

FIFI KNOWS ALL! FIFI CAN HELP! SHE CAN TAKE CARE OF YOUR TROUBLES FOR ONLY FIVE DOLLARS.

"No one can help me," Bonnie thought sadly, and she made her way home.

The phone was ringing as Bonnie opened the door. It was Helen, Bonnie's best friend. They were going out to eat together the next night.

"Bonnie," Helen started, "I know we were going to eat at the Captain's Table, but I don't feel like going there. Is it OK with you if we eat at the Gold Sword? I like the food there better."

Bonnie didn't like the food at the Gold Sword but she said, "It's OK with me."

"Good. See you then."

Bonnie put down the phone. She was not happy with herself. "I can't go on doing what other people want. I'd like to feel that what *I* want and what *I* think are important. There must be someone who can help me."

Then Bonnie remembered the sign in the store window.

FIFI KNOWS ALL! FIFI CAN HELP! SHE CAN TAKE CARE OF YOUR TROUBLES FOR ONLY FIVE DOLLARS.

"Why not give her a try?" Bonnie thought.

Bonnie ran out of her apartment and went right to Fifi's store.

Fifi didn't look at all the way Bonnie thought she would look. She was thin and beautiful. She had long, dark hair and a little turned-up nose. Fifi smiled at Bonnie and said, "Come in and sit down, dear." Bonnie liked her right away. She sat down and told Fifi everything.

"I see," Fifi said, when Bonnie was done. "You have nothing to worry about. I can fix everything."

Fifi handed Bonnie a little piece of wood. It had some writing on it that Bonnie couldn't read. "This piece of wood will help you," said Fifi. "It has a spell on it. As long as you keep it with you, you will feel that you are important, and you will have no trouble telling people what you think."

Bonnie looked at the piece of wood. "A spell," she thought to herself. "Why not? It could work. Maybe this is just what I need."

Bonnie gave Fifi five dollars and thanked her. "I hope it works," Bonnie said.

"Just believe in yourself, dear." Fifi waved as Bonnie left. Bonnie couldn't wait to try out the piece of wood.

The next morning, Bonnie put on her best dress and hurried out to work. When she got there, she went right in to see Ms. Lewis.

"Ms. Lewis, I'd like to talk to you about your sales plan. I think you're going to run into some trouble with it."

"Sit down, Bonnie, and we'll talk about it."

They talked about it, and Ms. Lewis was very happy with what Bonnie had to say. "I think your plan will save us a lot of money, Bonnie," said Ms. Lewis. "I'm glad you came to me."

Bonnie smiled. Fifi's piece of wood was doing its job.

At home that night, Bonnie was feeling very good. As she was getting ready to go out with Helen, there was a knock at the door. Helen was right on time.

"Hi, Bonnie. Are you ready to go?"

"Just about," Bonnie answered. Then she said, "Helen, I have something to say to you. I don't want to eat at the Gold Sword tonight. You always pick the places where we go to eat. I think it's time we went where I want to go."

"Bonnie, I didn't think you cared where we went. Of course, we'll eat wherever you want."

Bonnie had never been so happy. How had she ever lived without that piece of wood? She would show it to Helen.

But when Bonnie looked for the piece of wood, she couldn't find it. She started to feel afraid. Then she remembered. She had left it in the suit she was wearing when she went into Fifi's store. She hadn't had the piece of wood with her all day! But then what had made her talk to Ms. Lewis and to Helen the way she had? If not the piece of wood, then what?

Suddenly Bonnie knew the answer, and she was no longer afraid. She didn't need that piece of wood at all!

"You have a funny look on your face," said

Helen. "What were you looking for?"

"Nothing," Bonnie answered. "Nothing at all."

This happens every time I talk to it.

BLOOD:
Giving and Getting

Why is it so important to give blood?
Because blood saves lives.

Have you ever been asked to give blood? Someone may ask you to do this someday. Before you say yes or no, it's good to know something about giving blood.

You probably know why blood is always needed in hospitals. Every day, hundreds of people get hurt in accidents. Many other people are sick. Many of the hurt and sick people have lost a lot of blood. They need new blood right away. So at all times, hospitals must have lots of new blood on hand.

There is no way to "make" new blood for people. Blood can only come from other people. That is why someone may ask you to give blood someday. One woman never gave blood until her father got sick and needed blood. The hospital gave him the blood that he needed. After that, the woman gave blood as often as she could. It was her way of saying "thank you" for the blood that had saved her father.

The first time you give blood, you may be a little afraid. After all, people don't like to have needles put into them. But the needle doesn't hurt much, and it only takes a little time to give blood. You will be proud that you did it. The second time you give, you won't mind it at all.

The blood you give will go to a "blood bank." A blood bank is a place where blood is stored. It is often part of a hospital. Many people have been saved from death because a nearby blood bank had enough blood for them.

Blood will soon spoil if the blood bank doesn't keep it cold. Charles R. Drew (1904–1950) was an American doctor who studied ways to keep blood from spoiling. He worked with a team of doctors to find good ways to store blood. Around the time of World War Two, Dr. Drew helped set up many blood banks.

Dr. Drew did a lot of important work for blood banks. But even so, in the 1940s, some blood banks wouldn't take Dr. Drew's blood! Why? Because Dr. Drew was black.

But blood is blood. Black people can give blood to people who aren't black. And people who aren't black can give blood to black people. Today, blood banks take blood from everyone who will give it. The only thing that is important is that the giver is in good health.

There are 4 kinds of blood. The 4 kinds of blood are named by letters: A, B, AB, and O. Do you know which kind of blood you have? When you give blood, you'll find out.

If you ever get hurt and need blood, your doctor must find out which kind of blood you have. This is because the doctor may only give you more of your kind of blood. If she or he gives you another kind, you could get very sick.

Don't worry about it. There is a very easy way for a doctor to find out which kind of blood you have. Before you get any new blood, the doctor will see to it that you get the right kind.

If you want to give blood, you can do it. But you must be over 17, and you must be in good health. Remember: blood saves lives. People who give blood know that they have helped someone live.

Here are some good waker-uppers for the morning: Up . . . down . . . up . . . down. Now, the other eye.

Angela, Ray,
and Cloudy Day

**Ray was *too little* for Angela to see.
Then something happened to make him a *big* man
in Angela's eyes.**

The people on his street always said that Ray was
"a little slip of a boy" until he was a young man.
Then, when he was older, they said that he was "a
good-looking little man." They thought he was
smart, which he was, and they thought he was
good-looking. "But he's little," they said.

When Ray was old enough to start looking at girls,
he saw that the girls looked at other boys more than
they looked at him. He saw that the girls were more
attracted to the taller boys.

It had always hurt Ray that people had thought of
him just as being little. Now that Ray was a young
man, it still hurt. "There's more to a man than just
how tall he is," he thought. "Why can't people see
that?" Of course, when Ray said this, he was

thinking mostly about the young women he knew.

All of his friends had girl friends, but Ray did not. When Ray wanted to do something like go to a ball game, his friends wanted to go see some girls. True enough, he could go with them, but what good would it do? Ray knew that the girls wouldn't go out with him because he was "too little."

Then one day Ray saw Angela. Ray thought she was beautiful, and she was little, too. There was one trouble—Angela never saw him. When he saw her on the street, she didn't see him. When he saw her on the bus, she didn't see him. And when he was with his friends, she saw all of his friends—but she didn't see him. But one way or another, Ray thought, he was going to get Angela to see him. He had to.

About this time, Ray got a job working for a man, Mr. Homes, who owned some horses. Ray took care of the horses. One of the horses was named "Cloudy Day." Mr. Homes hoped that Cloudy Day would win first prize in a race that was coming up soon. Ray took good care of Cloudy Day, and he used to talk to her about Angela as he worked.

Ray also talked to Cloudy Day about the race. Ray liked to ride Cloudy Day to give her a work-out, and he knew she was a good, strong horse. He knew she would win. He thought of Cloudy Day as his own horse. But he knew that if Cloudy Day did not earn the prize, she would be sold.

At night, Ray would climb upstairs to his room, where he would think about how well Cloudy Day had run that day. It would kill him if she didn't win, he thought. Then Ray thought about Angela until he went to sleep.

Two days before the race, Mr. Homes came to talk to Ray.

"Ray," he said, "I want you to ride Cloudy Day in the race."

"Me?" Ray asked.

"You!" Mr. Homes said.

The man who was to have done the riding was sick. "Someone has to ride her!" Mr. Homes said. "And you and Cloudy Day get along so well."

"But I don't think I'm such a good rider," said Ray.

"You'll just have to try," said Mr. Homes.

And that was that. Ray said he would ride Cloudy Day, and he went to tell her so. He wondered what Angela would think if she knew he was going to ride in the race. That is, if she thought about him at all!

All of Ray's friends came to see the race. The prize was a big one—5000 dollars. And Ray knew that Cloudy Day would do her best. He talked to her quietly. "You're a real beauty," he said. "You'll win today. You've got to win!"

Then they were off! For part of the way, Ray was keeping Cloudy Day back. He wanted her to be strong all the way. Then, Ray said, "Let's go!" and he hit her lightly on her side. Cloudy Day took off! She moved past all the other horses, and when they came to the wire, Cloudy Day had won! They had won the prize! Ray was a happy man.

After the race, Ray was standing next to Cloudy

Day. People were all around them. His friends were all there. Just then, one of his friends came over to him with a girl. "Angela," the friend said, "meet my friend Ray."

Angela looked at him. "It's very good to meet you, Ray." She had a lovely smile. "I wonder why I never saw you before!"

Ray looked at Angela. He thought of all the times he had tried to meet her. And he thought of all the times she had never looked at him. "How do you do, Angela," Ray said. Then he said, "No, you never saw me before. I was there, but you never saw me."

Angela's smile was beautiful. She said to Ray, "Please come out with all of us tonight."

"What if I hadn't won?" Ray suddenly asked.

"What do you mean?" Angela said.

"Nothing," Ray said. He put his hand on Cloudy Day. "It's something to meet a girl like you, Angela," he said, "but I don't think I'll be able to go out with all of you tonight." Then he took Cloudy Day away, and he left Angela standing there.

"Isn't it strange?" Ray said to his horse. "I was always there. But she never saw me until I won a race! Well, there's more to a man than how tall he is. And there's more to being a man than winning races! One day, I'll meet a girl who sees me just for myself, and not because I've won a race!" And he didn't look back at Angela as he took Cloudy Day away.

Will Rogers

Here's a story about a man who knew his roping, knew his horses, and knew how to talk to people.

Have you ever seen a Wild West Show? Even if you haven't, you know there would be horses in it with good riders. There would be men and women who know how to rope a horse or a cow. You would see some of the best riders and ropers in the world at a Wild West Show.

One of the greatest ropers of all time was a man named Will Rogers. He was part American Indian. Though he was proud of his roping, he was prouder of his Indian blood. He told people over and over that his parents were part Indian.

Will was born near Claremore, Oklahoma, in 1879. He learned to use a rope while still a young boy. Later, he got better and better at it while working as a cowboy. Will did tricks with his rope.

He could stand still and rope a rider on a horse who was riding away from him! In another trick, he could use 3 ropes, and with them, rope a rider, the horse's head, and the horse's middle, all at one time!

Will was so good with a rope that he attracted the attention of show people. They signed Will up to work for them. Will Rogers went around America and to many places in the world, doing rope tricks in Wild West Shows. People loved him.

But Will did more than just rope tricks. While working in a show with his rope, Will talked. At first, he talked just to himself, keeping his voice down. He said funny things, and some people sitting near him could hear what he said. Everyone else wanted to hear, too, so Will started talking louder. He told jokes while he did his rope tricks.

Some of Will's jokes were about himself. Now and then, but not often, Will would miss one of his rope tricks. Then he would say, "I've only got jokes enough for one miss. I've got to be a better roper or else learn more jokes."

Will's jokes were funny, but they were more than funny. He said things that made people think. Even today, most of the things he said still make people think.

"I always like to hear a man talk about himself," Will said, "because then I never hear anything but good." That's the kind of talk people remember.

Soon more people came to hear Will talk than to watch his rope tricks. Will had a quiet, easy voice that had a lot of fun in it.

Will had a lot of funny things to say about the people who ran the country. "We spend three times as much money running the country today as we did 20 years ago. And the country isn't being run one bit better than it was then."

Will had a lot of things to say about war, too. "When you get into trouble 5000 miles from home, you've got to have been looking for it." Will also said, "You've got to believe that people have gotten smarter over the years . . . for in every war they kill you in a new way."

People knew that Will wasn't just trying to be funny when he said these things. They knew that he was saying things that were very true.

Will got to be well known, and he got started going around the world on his own. More and more people came to hear him talk. His rope tricks weren't so important anymore. People wanted Will to make them laugh. And Will wanted people to think about what he said.

People started hearing Will "on the air," and seeing Will in movies. He began to make good money. But he never forgot that he was "just a country boy." He cared about people. When times were very bad in the 1930s, Will went around the country getting money and food to help needy people.

Will Rogers died in 1935. He died in an air crash. Suddenly, the world was a sadder place.

People all over the country and the world loved Will Rogers. They loved him because he loved people and he loved to make them laugh. "I never met a man I didn't like," Will said. People everywhere knew that this was true. Even today, people smile when they think of him. The name "Will Rogers" will be remembered for a long time.

**The morning paper
has some strange news
for Joe.**

Read All about It

It was Monday morning. Joe Cory picked up the newspaper by his front door. He carried it to the table and sat down. As always, he turned first to the sports news. Joe was a catcher for a baseball team, the Cats, and he liked to read about his team in the paper.

Today, one story looked strange. It seemed to jump out at him from the newspaper. The story said, "Monday, May 7. The Cats beat the Wheels tonight, 5–3, on a home run by Willie Blake. Blake's home run came with two men on base in the last inning."

"This story is all wrong," thought Joe. "We didn't play the Wheels last night. We play them tonight. Last night, we played the Bees. We won,

1–0. And Willie Blake didn't hit a home run. This story is all wrong! This newspaper is nuts!"

Joe looked at the rest of the paper. All the other stories looked OK. Joe didn't understand how the newspaper could be so wrong. "Very strange," he thought. And then he forgot about it.

Later in the day, Joe drove out to the ballpark for the game.

The Cats got out in front, 2–0. But late in the game, the Wheels got three runs. Going into the last inning, the Cats were down, 3–2.

With one out, it was Joe's turn to bat. He got a base hit up the middle. The people in the stands came alive. And the next batter, Manny Miles, got a base hit to left. Joe pulled into second base and stopped. The people in the stands were shouting now: "Let's do it! Let's win this game, Cats!" And as Joe looked in from second base, he remembered the newspaper story he had read that morning.

"I can't believe it," thought Joe. "Everything is happening just like the story said." Willie Blake was at bat, and Willie crashed the ball deep into the stands. Joe said it out loud now: "I can't believe it!" Willie's home run won the game, just like the story had said.

After the game, all the Cats were happy. But Joe Cory was quiet. He drove home slowly. All the way, he was thinking, "Something very, very strange is going on."

When Joe got home, he looked at the newspaper again. But now the story was gone! In its place was the story of last night's game with the Bees! "Am I going out of my mind?" thought Joe. "Or am I under a spell? Or does my newspaper have a spell on it?"

Joe didn't sleep very well that night.

Tuesday morning, the newspaper was at the front door. Joe almost tore it open to the sports news. Again, one story looked strange. It said, "Tuesday night, Al Wood got the winning hit as the Cats beat the Wheels again." Joe thought, "Can this be true? Al's not much of a hitter. Well, we'll see tonight."

That night at the ballpark, Joe laughed as Al Wood's hit rolled all the way to the fence. The winning run came home, just like the paper had said. "What a lift to win like this again!" said Manny Miles. Joe smiled but said nothing.

Joe drove home, still smiling. "I must be under a spell," he thought. "I can make millions with that newspaper! Millions!" With that thought in his mind, Joe got home and went to sleep.

In the morning, the paper was at the front door. Standing there by the open door, Joe looked for the story right away. What would it say today?

Again, the story was about the game the Cats would play that day. But Joe's eyes saw only one part. It said: "Joe Cory, the young catcher, hurt his hand badly and is in the hospital. He won't be able to play for ten weeks."

"No!" said Joe. "It can't be! It *won't* be!" His hands were shaking. "I'll say I'm sick. If I don't play, I won't hurt my hand. It will be better to say

I'm sick than to play and hurt my hand!"

Afraid, Joe turned toward the kitchen. He started to shut the door. But he was still shaking. He let go of the door. The door crashed shut, catching his hand and cutting it deeply. Joe gave out a sickening cry.

The next morning, Joe sat in a hospital room. The morning newspaper was beside him. With his good hand, Joe turned to the sports news. "Maybe I can still make those millions," he thought. "I'll bet on the game!"

But no story told about today's game. The newspaper was just a newspaper. Joe's spell was over.

Ed: I have some good news for you and some bad news.

Ted: What's the good news?

Ed: NBC just loved your story, just ate it up.

Ted: That's great! Now, what's the bad news?

Ed: NBC happens to be my dog.

The Race:
A Fable for Our Time

Pat wanted to be the one to pick the man she would marry. So she ran the most important race of her life.

Pat was really angry at her father. "How can you tell me who to marry? I will pick my own man."

"It is for your sake that I do this, my child," her father said. "A young girl can't pick a man for herself."

"But how will *you* pick someone?" Pat asked.

Her father told her about the race. "All the young men in our village will run a race. The fastest man will earn the right to marry you."

Pat's father traced the course that the runners would take. On a small map of the village he showed Pat the lake.

"Here is where they will start. They will run next to the lake until they get to this old stable. There they will turn right and go up this street. At the end of the street is Mr. Clay's chicken house. They must go inside the house and get an egg from Mr. Clay's pail to show that they have been there. Then they will turn around and run back to the lake."

"When will all this happen?" asked Pat.

"In six weeks, my child. This is how it has always been done. Your mother's father and her mother's father before that have given their children's hand in this way. And that is how I will give yours. Don't you worry about it."

But Pat was worried. It was just not fair. She wanted no part of her father's race. She would not be a prize for any man.

Suddenly, Pat knew what she was going to do. She would win the race herself!

This was her plan: Every morning Pat would wake up before anyone else in her family. Then, while the rest of the village slept, she would run the course.

Pat was a very fast runner. But the first time she ran the course, she was slow. And by the time she got to Mr. Clay's, she had a pain in her side. It was a long way, and she wasn't used to running that far.

After a while, though, Pat saw that she could run faster. She was stronger, too. Each time it was as if the long course got a little shorter than the time before. "No man will catch me," Pat thought. "And then I will be able to marry the man I want!"

On the day of the big race, Pat's father said, "Come with me to the lake, my child. Don't you want to meet the man who comes in first?"

"No, Dad. I'll stay here if you don't mind. I told

you I don't want any part of this race.''

"Suit yourself," said her father as he walked out the door.

When her father was out of sight, Pat dressed in her brother's clothes. When she put her long hair up under a hat, she looked like a young man. "This is the only other thing I need," she said as she put an egg into her coat. "Now I'm ready to win."

When she got to the lake, Pat couldn't believe how many men were there. She took her place with the others. No one knew she was really a young woman.

Go! A gun shot, and they were off, each "man" racing as fast as "he" could. They ran and ran, past the lake and toward the stable. At first they all stayed together. But soon three runners took the lead.

When the three got to Mr. Clay's chicken house, only two went inside. A young man in a hat started running back to the lake before the others. It looked as if he would win the right to marry Pat.

Pat's father was there to meet him. The runner gave him an egg from his coat.

"Son," he said as he shook the young man's hand, "you have earned the right to marry my girl."

"No, Father. I have earned the right to pick my own man." With that, Pat took off her hat and let her long hair fall out.

"Pat! It's you! You ran in the race. I can't believe you raced every young man in this village. How did you do it?"

Pat told her father about running the course every **morning while the village slept.**

"You really wanted to win, didn't you?" Her father put his arm around her.

"No, Dad, I really wanted to show you that a fast runner may not be the best person for me to marry."

In time, Pat did marry a young man from the village. But it was someone she picked for herself. She never told her father about hiding the egg in her coat. Even though it had helped her win, Pat believed she probably would have won anyway. After all, it was too important a race to have lost.

Someone Else's Watch

Finders may be keepers, but Cerita just wasn't happy until she got rid of the watch she had found.

It was a beautiful watch, on a long, thin, gold watchband.

Cerita saw it on her way out of work. It lay on the floor, between a table and a chair. Slowly, she picked it up and looked at it. The watch was very old. On the front was a stone, set in a gold rim. On the back were the letters HGB for someone's name. Cerita was sure it would be easy to find the owner.

She turned it over in her hand. A little noise drew her attention. Holding the watch up, she listened. It ticked quietly. What a lovely thing it was.

Who could have lost it? Really, such a watch needed an owner who would take more care of it. It needed an owner who would treat it well.

Suddenly, Cerita wanted the watch. After all, she had been the only one to see it. Other people had

41

walked right by it as it lay there on the floor.

"Finders keepers," said Cerita, remembering the old saying. Turning to see if anyone was looking, she slipped the watch into her coat. Then she hurried from the building.

At home, Cerita looked at the watch for a long time. Then, slowly, she tried it on. It looked great. She turned it this way and that. Yes, the watch suited her. It was funny, though, how the ticking noise was louder here in her room. Cerita took off the watch and put it neatly in her dresser.

That night she was sure she could hear the watch ticking in her dresser. She couldn't get over how loudly it ticked.

In the morning Cerita was up early. She did not have to work that day and she could have slept late. But something was on her mind. She thought she had heard the watch ticking in her sleep.

Cerita took the watch out of her dresser. It was even more pleasing to look at in the morning light. She got dressed and slipped the watch on over her hand. She would wear it when she went out on her bicycle.

Outside, Cerita smiled. It was a real spring day, sunny, but not too hot, not too cold, the kind of day Cerita liked best. She climbed on her bicycle and headed downtown to do some shopping.

She rode fast, her hair blowing, the air hitting her face. It was a good feeling. It was a good day . . . almost.

In the first store the salesman showed her some rings.

"This one would go well with your watch," he said. "See how attractive it would be. . . ."

Cerita dropped the ring suddenly and looked at the watch. There it was, ticking away, louder than ever.

"Remember, it's yours now," she told herself. Still, she was in a hurry to leave the store. Maybe the salesman had seen this watch before.

In another shop someone asked her the time. Cerita jumped. "I don't know," she said. Then she heard the ticking again. "Oh! Oh, yes, it's, let's see. . . ." Her voice shook as she told the time. Why had *she* been asked in the first place? Were people looking for the watch?

Cerita took the fast road home. The thin, gold watchband was heavy, and her head hurt from the noise that never stopped. Tick . . . tick . . . tick. . . .

"I'll take it off for a while," she told herself. "I'll wear it later when I go out again."

That night Cerita went to the movies. But it was hard to hear the movie. Her watch ticked so loudly.

Cerita went home early.

That night, Cerita put the watch in her closet. But its noise followed her to bed. She didn't sleep well at all.

In the morning, she didn't take the watch out. She didn't wear it all day Sunday. She couldn't wait for Monday.

On Monday Cerita put the beautiful watch in a box and took it to work.

"Someone lost a watch," she said. "It was on the

floor near this table."

A woman came up right away. Cerita didn't know her well. The woman said, "Was it an old watch, with the letters HGB on one side?"

Cerita said "Yes."

"It was my mother's," the woman said. She took the watch from Cerita and put it on. "Thank you so much!" Her voice was happy and her eyes were smiling. "I lost it," she went on, "but I knew it was in good hands. It was as if I could hear it ticking for the past two days."

Cerita didn't say too much. It hurt to give back the watch. But at last she couldn't hear it ticking anymore. The noise was gone from inside her head.

"It was a beautiful watch," Cerita said to herself. "But it was someone else's."

He: Our dog is just like one of the family.
She: Really? Which one?

The Wonder of the Moon

Even though we know a lot about the moon, people will probably always wonder about it.

People have always loved to watch the moon as it sails across the dark sea of night. Lovers take walks in the moonlight. Storytellers write about the beauty of the moon. For people everywhere, the moon has always been a great wonder.

But now some of the wonder is gone. We have learned a lot about the moon. In 1969, two American men were the first people to land on the moon. So today we know a lot about it.

What do we know? We know that the moon is very hot where the sun shines on it. It is much hotter than earth. But the moon is also much colder than the earth where the sun is not shining on it. Because of the heat and the cold, there is probably no life on the moon. And there is no food or water on the moon.

The moon may look to you like a friendly face. Some people call it the "man in the moon." We know that there are mountains and craters on the moon. These mountains and craters are what look like the face of the "man in the moon."

The sun, of course, is very bright, and the moon is not so bright as the sun. The sun gives off its own light, but the moon doesn't. All of the moon's light comes from the sun. Sunlight shines on the moon, and then the moon shines this light down on the earth. You can see how this works by holding a looking glass up to the sun. Let the sunlight shine on the glass. Then move the looking glass and send the sunshine from it to other places. The moon acts like the looking glass. It sends sunshine down to earth. But we call it moonlight.

You may know that the sun shines on only half of the earth at any one time. The other half of the earth is dark at that time. This is why we have day and night. In the same way, the sun shines on only half of the moon at any one time, and the other half of the moon is dark. When we look at the moon, we can see only the part of the moon that is being lighted by the sun.

It takes the moon about one month to move around the earth. On the night when the lighted half of the moon faces away from the earth, you cannot see the moon at all. The next night, you will see a small, thin piece of the moon. Each night after that, you will see a little more of the moon. Each night you will keep on seeing another thin piece until, after about one week, the moon looks like this:

This is called a "half moon."

By the end of the second week, you will be able to see the round, full moon. When the moon is "full," you can see all of the face of the "man in the moon."

At the end of three weeks, you will see only the half moon again. Look at it now.

In what way has it changed from the half moon of two weeks before?

At the end of the month you cannot see the moon at all. Now, once again, the lighted half of the moon is facing away from the earth. A new "moon month" is starting, and we have what we call a "new moon."

Not too many years ago, the moon seemed very strange to us. But we know so much about it now that it no longer seems strange. 12 Americans have walked on the moon. There's even a chance that people may one day be living on a "moon base."

Yes, much of the wonder about the moon is gone. But the beauty of the moon is still there. Storytellers will still write about it, and lovers will always hold hands in the moonlight. Don't you think so?

No One Lives Forever

What is it that Ellen is hiding from everyone? Will the man in the large, shiny car find out?

The auto came slowly along the dirt road and stopped by the fence in front of Ellen's house. It was a large, shiny car, heavy and proud like a well-dressed banker. It sat there for a second, started to move, and then stopped again.

Ellen looked out the kitchen window. She saw a ray of sunlight shine like silver on the side of the car. The light was so bright that she couldn't see anyone inside the car. For some seconds more, she waited, watching. Then, she went to the front door, opened it, and went outside.

Ellen walked across the open ground between the house and the fence. As she went past the fish pond, some ducks ran to get out of her way. Ellen came slowly up to the fence and looked at the car. She could see better now. A man with dark glasses was sitting at the steering wheel, and the back windows of the car were covered.

Ellen stood at the fence, watching the driver. But he just sat there. Seconds went by. Now, for the first time, Ellen thought, "Maybe I should have stayed inside the house."

At last the driver's window opened. Ellen heard a voice say, "Good day." But it wasn't the driver who was talking. It was someone else, someone sitting in the back of the car.

"Good day," Ellen answered. "Lost?"

"Let's see," said the voice. "Is this the old Harding place?"

"No, it's not," Ellen said. "That's down the road. About ten miles."

"Did you hear that, Andrew?" said the voice.

"Yes, I heard," said the driver. "Down the road. About ten miles."

The driver rolled up his window.

Ellen thought she heard someone say, "Thank you," but she wasn't sure. And slowly, without a noise, the big car started to move.

"It will be on your left," Ellen called out. "The Harding place!" But by now the car was down the road, and a second later, it was gone.

Ellen sat by the fish pond for the rest of the day. The water was clean and cold and beautiful, just like it had been for hundreds of years. Ellen was singing an old, old song. The song went, "You can't live forever, not even if you try. You can't live forever;

someday, you'll have to die."

Then Ellen looked around her. "I do love this old farm," she thought. "I couldn't bear to leave it, ever."

Ellen leaned over the clean, still water of the pond. A fish came up to the top. Then it turned quickly and shot away. Ellen took a long, long drink from the water. "Thank you, little fish pond," she said. "Thank you for your life-giving water." Then she got slowly up and walked back to the house.

The next day, the big, shiny car was back. It sat in the road, just where it had sat the day before. But this time a man was standing beside it. He was old, but he was dressed like a man who had money. Lots of money.

When he saw Ellen, he stepped past the fence and walked slowly toward her. Ellen stopped. He came up to her, and he looked in her face.

"You tricked me," he said.

Ellen knew his voice. She had heard it the day before. It was the voice that had come from the back of the car.

"You tricked me," he said again. "*This* is the Harding place."

Ellen looked back at him. "I didn't trick you. The Harding place is down the road."

"No!" he said. "*This* is the Harding place. You have tricked many people for many years. But with my money, I can find out anything I want. And now I know that this is the Harding place."

Ellen said nothing.

"You are Ellen Harding," the man said. Suddenly he looked very sad. And very old. "I am old," he said. "I don't want to die."

"I know," said Ellen.

He went on, "I met a man once. He knew you many years ago. He told me to find the old Harding place. He said Ellen Harding *will live forever.*"

"That is not true," said Ellen.

He kept talking. "My pain is great. I am old. But I have money. I will pay anything. Please! Tell me how to live forever! I don't want to die!" With that, he sank to the ground.

Ellen looked down at him. "Go away," she said. "Go away!"

He went away.

That night, Ellen came to the fish pond once again. "Now they know," she thought. "Now everyone will know. They will come here again. And so it is time for me to leave, after all these years."

Ellen dropped the little cake of poison into the fish pond. "That's all," she thought. "Good-bye, my little fish pond. Your life-giving waters are poison now. No one can drink them anymore. No one will live forever!"

Ellen Harding, 275 years old, turned and walked away from the fish pond. Forever.

When something is wrong people can just take it or they can do something about it.

Carlos thinks it is time to do something.

Carlos Speaks Up

"I've had it!" said Carlos. "Six men from this machine shop have gone to the hospital this year. It's got to stop." As he talked, he pounded the table with his fist. The other workers listened but they said nothing. Carlos Martinez was asking for trouble—and they wanted none of it.

"How long will we just sit here and take it? We must fight back!"

At last, one of the older men said something. "Carlos, you're right. But there's nothing we can do. I'm a poor man. I need this job more than they need me. If I quit, they'll just find another man to take my place."

"I'm not telling you to quit," said Carlos. "I'm telling you to speak up. Just because you're poor, it doesn't mean that you're dumb or that your life has to be in danger."

52

Carlos could tell that the others knew he was right. But they were all afraid.

He went on. "Look, my child Maria goes to school with your children. Do you know what they learn? To speak up for their rights! Our 12-year-olds are smarter than we are!"

"So go ask *her* for help, if she's so smart!" The men laughed.

"Listen! Maria told me that if the boss won't do anything, there are people in the government who will. Their job is to keep workers safe and to make sure that their health is not in danger."

Just then, they heard the bell. The coffee break was over. The men went back to work and Carlos was left standing by himself. "If they won't do it with me, I'll do it myself," Carlos thought.

That night Carlos talked to his family about his plan. "What's the name of that government office you told me about, Maria?"

"It's called OSHA, Dad. The letters stand for Occupational Safety and Health Administration."

"I'm going to call them," said Carlos.

"No, not now," said Maria. "First you must talk to your boss. My teacher said that a worker should give his boss a chance to make changes. If the worker still thinks his health is in danger, then he should call OSHA."

Mrs. Martinez looked at her husband. "I'm afraid," she said. "I wish you would think about this first."

"I have thought about it," Carlos said. "Now it is time to act."

Carlos got to work before eight the next day. He went right to his boss's office.

"Mr. Block, the machine shop isn't safe. Many of the machines don't work right. Men get hurt. Gas escapes from the pipes. It chokes us. It's as if we're being poisoned a little every day."

"Listen, Carlos, I'm glad you've come to see me. I've known you only a short time, but you seem like a good worker. I'll see what I can do. But remember, I don't own this place. I only run it. This may be out of my hands."

"I hear what you're saying, Mr. Block, but I don't care. All the time we get the same answer: 'We'll see.' Well, I'm willing to give you a few weeks, but that's all."

"And then what?" Now Mr. Block began to get angry. He didn't like the way Carlos was talking to him. "I told you I'd look into it. Now get out of here before I get really angry."

One week went by, and that turned into two. Before Carlos knew it, it had been a month since he had talked with Mr. Block. Things were no better. There were more accidents. One time a machine went up in flames. Some men were hurt. None of it would have happened if the machines had been fixed.

Carlos called the OSHA office. The woman on the phone told him to come in and tell her what was happening at work.

The next day, Carlos went to the OSHA office. The woman asked many questions. Carlos told his story, and she wrote everything down. Sometimes she asked him to spell someone's name or to talk a little more slowly.

"I think that OSHA can help you, Mr. Martinez. We'll send someone over to check your workplace and to talk to your boss. If we find that the machines aren't safe and that the workers are in danger, we'll do something about it."

"Can you *make* them change things?" asked Carlos.

"That's what we're here for. That's why the government set up this office. If your boss or the people who own the place don't make the changes we ask for, they may have to pay a fine. We can even make them close down until they do what we ask."

Carlos couldn't believe it. He had found help after all.

Within a week, a man from OSHA came to the job. He walked around checking things for an hour or so. Then he talked with Mr. Block for a long time. Carlos and the other men wondered what would happen.

More weeks passed by. Nothing happened right away. But soon there were changes. The machines were fixed. Some windows that had been covered with boards now had glass in them. The place was brighter. There were still a few accidents here and there, but things were much better than they had ever been.

Carlos never said a word to anyone about his call to OSHA. But everyone knew he had something to do with the changes.

One day Mr. Block called for Carlos. "Martinez, I don't know for sure, but I think you're the one who called that OSHA man."

Carlos was worried. He thought he might get fired.

Suddenly, Mr. Block smiled. "I'm not angry, Carlos. I was at first. But now I'm glad you sent for that OSHA man. You were right. The men are happier now, so they work better. The changes were good for all of us."

Mr. Block shook Carlos' hand. "You're going to get ahead in this world, Carlos, because you're willing to speak up for yourself."

Carlos closed the door, smiled, and thought, "It took a 12-year-old girl to teach a man how to speak up."

After the bank had been robbed by the same man for the third time, the policeman asked the teller, "Was there anything you saw about this man that we should know?"

"Yes," said the teller. "He looked better dressed each time."

THE WORLD TRADE CENTER

What would it be like to stand at the top of one of the world's tallest buildings and look down? It's a top-of-the-world feeling!

Have you ever stood at the top of the world? If you're ever in New York City, you might want to see the two tall buildings of the World Trade Center. They are each 1,350 feet high, and they each have 110 floors! If you go to the buildings, you must go to the top. You'd never guess what a wonderful feeling it is to be so high up.

Each of the two buildings has more than 120 elevators. But, in each building, only three elevators go all the way to the top. It takes 58 seconds to ride from the ground floor to the 107th floor. From there you must ride on a moving stairway up to the 110th floor. Then, hold on, and be ready for a wonderful sight! You just may feel as if you're standing on top of the world.

On a good day you can see almost all of the city, its buildings, parks, and streets. Looking west, you can see far into New Jersey. Looking south, you can see out to the Atlantic Ocean.

Nothing looks the same as it does when you're down in the street. The other buildings of New York look like doll houses. The people on the sidewalks look like bits of dust, moving ever so slowly. The cars in the streets look like toys.

It's very quiet at the top. You're so high up that the sounds of the busy city can't get to you. The sounds get lost somewhere, down in the streets.

When you're ready to come down, you might want to look around inside the buildings. The two buildings are so big that they have enough room for all the people of a very big town. More than 30,000 people work there every day. And there is room for 20,000 more. Another 20,000 people come every day just to see the buildings. These buildings are so big that 500 people have to come every evening just to clean up!

So that all of these people can come and go easily, there are underground trains that stop right in the heart of the World Trade Center. There are also parking places underground for 2,000 cars.

If there is anything that a person might need, you can bet that it's at the World Trade Center. There are stores of all kinds, banks, hairdressers, and places to eat. You could almost live all of your life there without ever going outside of the buildings!

The World Trade Center seems to be a good place

to work. But many of the people who work there aren't happy about it. Some of them don't like being so high up in the air. At times they feel sick when they look down from their windows. One woman says that she doesn't like the clean, "cold" feeling of the place. Like many new office buildings, the World Trade Center seems to be missing a "personal" feeling. Maybe that is because the buildings make people feel so small.

However, many people believe that the World Trade Center is a good thing for New York City. It's easy to get to, they say. They also say that a lot of money is saved by having so many workers in one place. But that's something that can never be known for sure.

Whatever anyone says, the World Trade Center is there to stay. The buildings took more than 7 years to finish. They cost nearly 800 million dollars. They will probably stand for hundreds of years.

To many people, these tall buildings are beautiful. From far away, they look like two long arms going up to the clouds. A few years ago, a tight-rope walker did his act on a rope between the two buildings! He was 1,350 feet in the air, all alone, high up over New York. He was walking at the top of the world.

A HOME FOR ANNA

Bob and Janet are on their way to see Anna, a little girl they hope will live with them. But there's danger on the road. Help comes to them in a strange way.

"I think we're lost, Bob," said Janet Moore as she studied the directions she was holding.

"We can't be," answered her husband. "I've been following Ms. Stanton's directions. Besides, how can you tell? There's so much fog that I can't see two feet in front of the car."

Janet looked up. The fog covered everything. They had wanted to see Anna so badly that they hadn't listened to the weather before starting out that morning.

Janet remembered when she first got the call from Ms. Stanton. "Mrs. Moore, I have something wonderful to tell you," she had said. "We have a little girl who needs a home. She's eight years old. I know that you and Mr. Moore wanted a baby, but I wish you would come to see Anna. She's a beautiful child. I know you would be good for each other."

Janet and Bob had wanted to see Anna right away. Ms. Stanton told them that Anna was staying at a home with other children out in the country. She gave Janet directions and said she would meet them there tomorrow. It was a long drive, so Janet and Bob had started out early. Now it was almost night and they were still driving.

"Where do I turn next?" Bob asked as he turned to face Janet.

"Watch out!" she cried. "There's somebody in the road!"

Bob made a short stop. In the car lights, he saw a woman. She seemed to come out of no where. As soon as the car stopped, she walked over to Bob.

"Thanks for stopping," she said. "I didn't know any other way to stop a car. No one could see me in this fog. My car died on me down the road. Can you give me a lift?"

The woman was very attractive, with big dark eyes and long brown hair. There was something strange about her, but Bob couldn't say just what it was. To her he said, "Sure. Get in."

Bob opened the back door for her. As she sat down, she said, "My name is Angela."

"I'm Bob and this is Janet. Where can we take you?"

"Well, I think the nearest gas station is in Plainfield. Is that out of your way?"

"Not at all," answered Janet. "We're headed that way, too. We're going there to see a child. Her parents are both dead, so she needs a home. We hope to have her live with us."

Angela smiled. "I think you'll make wonderful parents."

Janet then turned her attention back to the directions. "I think if you just keep going the way you're headed, you'll come to Route 27," she told Bob. "That should take us into Plainfield."

"No!" came a strange cry from the back of the car. It made Bob's hair stand on end. "Don't take Route 27," Angela said. "I know these roads. It would be better to take I-17 into town. Just bear right at the next traffic light."

"But Ms. Stanton's directions say to take Route 27," Janet said.

"Please listen to me. You must not take Route 27."

Something in Angela's voice made Janet afraid. She turned to look at her. As Angela's eyes met hers, Janet was no longer afraid. She knew that Angela was right.

"Bob, bear right at the next light. We're taking I-17," Janet said.

"But you said..."

"Never mind what I said. Please take I-17."

"All right. You're the boss."

The car turned onto I-17. The three people in it didn't talk for the rest of the trip. When they drove into Plainfield, Angela asked to be let off at the first gas station they came to. As she left the car, she said, "Thanks for the lift. I wish you and Anna all the best." Then she walked away toward the station.

"That's funny," Janet thought. "We never told her the child's name was Anna."

They drove on and followed Ms. Stanton's directions to the home. Janet was jumpy. Would they like Anna? Would she like them?

When they knocked, Ms. Stanton opened the door and showed them into the living room. "I'm so glad you're all right," she said. "I just heard that there was a very bad accident on Route 27. Many people died. Did you see it?

Janet tried to stop herself from shaking. "No," she answered. "We took I-17. Can we see Anna now?"

"Of course. I'll get her." Ms. Stanton left the room.

Janet and Bob looked at each other. They were thinking the same thing: How did Angela know?

Soon Ms. Stanton came in with Anna. Janet and Bob were in love with her right away. She was very pretty. Beautiful dark eyes looked up at them out of a small round face. She was holding something in her right hand.

Janet walked over to her. "Anna, my name is Janet and this is Bob. We would like to get to know you. Then if you like us, you can come to live in our house. Would you like that?"

"Oh, yes," said Anna. "My mother wants me to live with you. She says you're going to be my new parents."

"Your mother?"

"Mrs. Moore, can I talk to you for a second?" Ms. Stanton cut in.

Janet walked to the side of the room with Ms. Stanton. "Anna's mother died in a plane crash five months ago," Ms. Stanton told her. "Anna still believes that her mother talks to her. She carries a picture of her mother with her all the time."

"I see," said Janet. "Poor thing. We'll give her the love she needs to get over this." When Janet went back to Anna, she asked her, "Can I see the picture of your mother?"

"I guess so," the girl answered and she handed Janet the picture.

Janet and Bob couldn't believe their eyes when they looked at the picture. There was Angela's face smiling up at them.

They Don't Make Them Like That Anymore

A fire! Should Maggie save her clock or Tommy, her cat? Or is there something even more important?

On most winter nights, Maggie Carson's apartment was ice-cold. Tonight there was lots of heat. "For once, I won't be cold," thought Maggie as she climbed into bed.

Maggie had lived alone on the top floor of the old building for many years. Her husband had been dead a long time. Her children had families of their own now, and they lived far away.

Maggie wasn't really all by herself, though. She lived with her cat, Tommy. Of course, there were other families in the building, too. Each year there seemed to be more children playing in the hallway and more toys left near the back stairs. But Maggie never really got to know the other families. Tommy the cat was her only real friend.

Maggie's old, silver clock said 11:15. The clock had been in her family for years. Maggie was always a little afraid the clock would stop one day and her life would stop with it. "How silly!" Maggie thought. She smiled as she fell asleep. She and the clock and the old building had all seen better days, she said to herself. But they would all be there in the morning.

That was the last thing Maggie remembered before the fire.

The smell of smoke made Maggie wake up. Then she heard fire trucks outside the building. "A fire!" she thought. Maggie jumped out of bed and grabbed for her clothes and her glasses. "I must hurry!" she said, as Tommy ran under the bed.

Just before she ran to the door, Maggie saw her old, silver clock. "If there's one thing I must save, it's that clock." She picked it up and headed for the door.

Maggie opened her door and went into the hallway. But heavy smoke rolled up all around her. It got into her eyes and nose, and she started choking. Her glasses slipped off and fell. Maggie could hear the glasses break as they hit the floor. "Oh no!" said Maggie as she got down on the floor to look for them. "What will I do? What will I do?" Just then, a splinter of glass cut Maggie's hand. The pain shook her, and suddenly, she stopped.

"What am I doing?" she thought. "Trying to save a clock? Am I crazy?" The clock belonged to the past and the past was dead and **gone. She was still** alive. And so was Tommy! "Tommy? Where is Tommy?"

Calling her pet's name, Maggie ran back into the apartment. Tommy tried to hide. Somehow, she was able to get him into his carrying box. She stepped back into the hallway with her pet, leaving the clock on the floor.

There was very little time. Maggie knew that. She had to get down the back stairs before the fire closed them off. Without her glasses, she could hardly see. But somewhere in the thick, black smoke was the stairway.

Maggie was afraid now. Could she make it down the stairs? Would the firemen climb all the way to the top floor to save her? Maybe no one knew she was here! Maggie's life dashed before her eyes. In her mind, the hands of the old clock came slowly to a stop.

Then suddenly, with her poor eyesight, Maggie saw a basket by the top of the stairs. There was something inside. Maggie came closer. It was a baby! Maybe the people next door were overcome by the smoke and had lost their baby!

Suddenly, Maggie knew what she must do. "I love you dearly, Tommy," she said. "But I can't carry you both. You're only a cat. A person's life is worth more than yours."

Maggie set down the carrying box, opened it, and let Tommy out. Then she picked up the small basket with the baby inside.

"Make your own way, **Tommy,**" she called out.

"Save yourself if you can!" With a little cry, Maggie turned and went down the back stairs.

When the firemen did find Maggie, they took her outside and took the basket away from her. They told Maggie they were sending her to the hospital. "Don't worry about me," said Maggie. "Save the baby."

Maggie's neighbors shook their heads as though they couldn't believe what they saw. "Did you see what old Maggie had in her arms?" one man said. "A doll! One of those new dolls that look like the real thing! Why would anyone want to save useless junk like that?"

Two hours later, the fire was out. It never got up to the top floor. When it was safe to go back inside, a fireman went upstairs with Maggie's neighbors.

The first thing they saw was the carrying box at the top of the stairs. Then Tommy the cat came out of hiding. He nosed around in the mess in the hallway. The fireman found Maggie's broken glasses and held them up.

"Now I see what happened. Come over here," he said. "In all the smoke, without her glasses, Maggie couldn't see. She didn't know she was carrying a doll. She really thought she was saving the life of a child. Believe me, I know. When you're afraid, you can go half-crazy. A doll can look like a real baby!"

Maggie's neighbors began to understand what had happened. One woman patted Tommy's head and said she would feed him until Maggie got back. Another looked at the old, silver clock. She smiled when she saw it was still running.

"They don't make them like that anymore," she said as she shook her head sadly.

"Like Maggie?" the fireman said. "No, they sure don't."

When your mind stops working, don't forget to turn off the sound.

FiRESTORM

The year was 1908, and the fire was very real. But people still don't know what it was or where it came from.

The year was 1908. The place was Siberia, a part of Russia. Early on the morning of June 30, something raced down out of the sky. Nearer and nearer toward Earth it came. Then flames lit up the whole sky. A ball of fire shot down to Earth. Suddenly, it hit—deep in the forest, in the place called Siberia.

A noise, loud enough to wake the dead, broke across the land. In a few seconds, hundreds and hundreds of trees came crashing down. In a short while, over 1,200 square miles of forest was knocked down or burned. But in one place, trees were left standing with only their tops splintered off. No one knew what had happened, but from that day on, people called it the "firestorm."

It was lucky that the firestorm hit Siberia and not someplace else. It was lucky because Siberia is a cold land with few cities and few people. It is covered by forests and ice. If the firestorm had hit another part of the world, many people probably would have been killed or hurt.

Few people lived near where the firestorm hit. Most who did were afraid to talk about it. Those who did talk told fearful stories.

"The forest was burning all around us," said one person. "Hundreds of trees were knocked down. There was also a great noise, like hundreds of guns going off at once."

Another said, "The storm was so bad that you couldn't stand up in it. Trees near our hut came crashing down."

People saw and heard the firestorm many miles away. In a town 40 miles away, people had to hide their faces from the heat. Windows crashed, roofs slipped off, animals ran every which way. Even 375 miles away, a whole train was shaken to a stop.

Still, no one knew where the firestorm had come from. In 1908 no one tried to find out.

Years went by. Word of the firestorm got around. In 1921 a man named L. Kulik heard about it. Kulik knew a lot about shooting stars. He believed the firestorm could have been caused by a shooting star from outer space. He wanted to visit Siberia to see where the firestorm had been. But his chance did not come until 1927. This was 19 years after the firestorm had happened.

Kulik went to Siberia. If a shooting star had crashed into Earth, it would have left a giant hole in the ground. So Kulik started looking for that hole.

The going was not easy. Kulik and his men had many problems. Heavy snow made the work hard and unsafe. There were few animals to be caught for food. Often the men were sick because there was so little to eat. And Kulik and his men didn't find any signs of a giant hole.

Over the years, Kulik made many visits to Siberia. But he never did find the hole. There just wasn't any.

On his visits, Kulik talked to many people. He listened to their stories. When he went into the forests, he wrote down everything he saw. But Kulik never learned where the firestorm had come from. He died in 1942 with no answers to his questions.

By this time, all over the world, people had heard about the strange fire in Siberia. They wanted to know what had happened. What had caused it?

In 1945 something happened that made people start to wonder. An atomic bomb was dropped on Japan. In many ways this bomb was like the firestorm of Siberia. There was the same kind of sound, the same fireball in the sky, and the same burned-out land.

A few splintered trees were left standing in Japan, just as some had been in Siberia. In Japan these trees were right below where the bomb went off.

The plants that came up after the Siberian firestorm started growing in a much faster and wilder way than before. This was also known to happen in places where an atomic bomb had gone off.

In Siberia, animals got sick and had sores after the firestorm came by. In Japan, too, people and animals were sick and burned after the bomb.

It began to seem, then, that the firestorm had not been caused by a shooting star. The great fire seemed to be atomic! But how could this have happened in 1908? There were no atomic bombs in 1908. Not on Earth.

Not on Earth? Perhaps that was the answer! Some people began to think that a spaceship had come to Earth from another world. Maybe, they said, it had atomic fuel. Maybe, they said, it was out of control and was going to crash. And maybe, whoever was on board saved the lives of many people on Earth by crashing the ship into Siberia, a place where few people lived.

Could this be the answer to the question? Could a ship from another world have come to Earth in 1908? From where could it have come?

Will we ever know the real story of the firestorm?

◖ ◗

Did you hear about the man who was so dumb that he sat in a car wash for three hours because he thought it was raining too hard to drive?

The contest

The eye of a camera sometimes shows more than words can say. Sara is looking for just the right picture to say it all.

The young woman read the small ad over and over.

PHOTOGRAPHY CONTEST!
We're looking for pictures that catch the feeling of America long ago. Pictures may be black and white or color. 1st prize: $500.

Sara knew she had to enter. It was the chance she had been waiting for. She had taken a photography course as soon as she had gotten her new camera. Being a wife and mother wasn't enough for her anymore. Sara wanted to start something new. This contest was her chance to show what she had learned in the photography course.

But it wasn't as easy as she thought. It took Sara a few weeks just to get started. What, she wondered, would show the America of long ago? Unable to think of anything, she took long walks with her camera in and around the small New England town where she lived.

She visited places—the clock building in the middle of town, the sweet-smelling tea warehouse, the soldiers' and sailors' hospital on Spring Street. They were all old buildings, but they didn't really show the old America.

One day, Sara walked along the river, letting the turning road of water lead the way. The summer sun was just right for picture-taking. But Sara had nothing to shoot. She was afraid she'd never think of the right picture for the contest. She was almost ready to give up.

Suddenly, she heard a strange voice: "Hello, there!" Sara stopped and looked around. She was surprised to see how far she had walked. To her left was the river. And to the right, set far back from the water, was a small, gray house.

"Hello, there!" the voice called again. Sara saw two people sitting on the front porch. As she moved closer to the house, she saw that they were an old man and woman. The man sat quietly as the woman waved to Sara.

"Please don't pass by. We don't get many visitors in these parts," said the old woman.

Smiling, Sara came up to the house. "Lovely day," she said.

"Yes, it is," said the woman. "Sit down, dear."

Sara sat down on the porch steps. "This is a

beautiful little place, here by the river," she said.

"Yes," the woman said. "But it's good to see a new face now and then. It's hard for Pa here to get around, so we stay close to home."

As the woman talked, Sara could see that the old man was shaking. His head dipped down on his chest, and his thick, gray hair came over his face. Sara could tell from his large hands and arms that he had once been very strong. But he never stopped shaking.

The old woman talked louder. "Pa, this young woman came here to visit." The old man lifted his head for a second and smiled at Sara.

"We've been living in these parts since we were both children," said the old woman. "In those days, this country was new and clean. No one had to worry about dirty air or water. I try to remember how good it was then. Remembering makes my life a little easier."

Sara listened as the woman talked about how life used to be. Pa had been a blacksmith, and a good one at that. They had had lots of family and friends nearby.

"Now there are cars, not horses. People don't need blacksmiths anymore. Our family has grown up and our friends have moved away—or died."

The woman went inside and came back with some coffee for Sara. She went on: "There's no harm in change, mind you. But there comes a time when you just can't keep up. And when you're old, people forget about you. No one needs us anymore."

Sara looked into the old woman's eyes and said, "Don't say 'no one.' I think you can help *me*." She told them about the contest and asked if she could take pictures of them. "I see now that the America of long ago cannot be found in wood or stone. It is right here, in people like you."

She took over fifty pictures of the old people. In the camera's eye, Sara could see that she was right.

Weeks later, when she got a letter from the people who ran the contest, Sara's heart raced wildly. She had won first prize!

Sara went back to see the old people. "I couldn't have done it without you," she told them. "So I'd like to give you part of the money I won."

"No, child! You can't go giving money away like that. You and those pictures of yours earned it. Besides, we don't need money."

"Please," said Sara, "there must be something I can do for you."

"Yes, dear, there is. Don't forget us. Come back and sit with us every now and then. But keep the money for new cameras. And keep taking pictures. You'll get even better at it."

Sara said she would be back. And in the end, she knew that they all had won what they needed.

My Job at The Animal House

What would it be like to work with animals all day long? Here is a story of the ups and downs of a person with a job like that.

I work for The Animal House. It's a place that takes care of animals that are lost, sick, or unwanted.

The Animal House takes in homeless animals and tries to find new homes for them. People who are looking for pets come to us for animals. We have dogs, cats, puppies, kittens, and birds. Once we even had a bear.

We also have a hospital for animals that are sick and hurt. The hospital takes all kinds of animals. We have two "vets," or animal doctors. That's what I want to be some day. I'm saving money to go to vet school.

One of my jobs is to find lost animals. Cats are always getting up into trees, and then they have trouble getting down. Sometimes I have to climb some very tall trees. Once I get up there, I have to talk the cat into coming to me. That's not always easy, but somehow most animals know that I care about them.

The hardest job I ever had was the night some monkeys got into the ball park. There were just five monkeys, but it seemed like there were fifty. They ran all over the field. They ran up and down the aisles and under the seats. Boy, I bet I ran up and down every aisle in the place trying to catch them. Some of them hid under the seats. This went on all night. But by morning I had caught them all. We didn't know where they had come from, so we took them to the zoo.

I like my job, but I sometimes have trouble keeping my cool. One thing that makes me angry is when people keep large animals in small apartments. I know a woman who has a Great Dane. Biggest dog I ever saw. I keep telling her it's not suitable to keep such a big dog in a two-room apartment. She says she lives near a park, and that her dog gets to run more than lots of dogs that live in the country. Well, if she's happy and the dog is happy, maybe I should keep quiet.

Another thing that makes me angry is the mess that dogs make on city sidewalks. It's not fair to the people who have to use the sidewalks. More and more dog owners are beginning to understand that it's their job to clean up after their own dogs. It's about time.

If you want to see me blow my top, ask me about

puppies and kittens. There's nothing I like more than baby animals. But lots of people don't want to care for the baby animals after a little while. If they can't find homes for them, they bring them here to The Animal House. You wouldn't believe how many puppies and kittens we get every year.

Most people know what to do about this. They can have their dogs and cats "fixed" so they can't have puppies and kittens. But the people don't want to spend the money. And some of these people care so little about animals that they'll leave young kittens out on the street to die. If I could get my hands on those people. . . .

Well, let's look at the bright side of my job. Did I tell you about the time I had to catch a fox?

This fox lived in an apartment, but it escaped. How about that—keeping a fox in a city apartment! Some people sure do crazy things.

It was a cold winter day. The fox was having a great time jumping around in the snow. But it slipped on some ice and I dropped a net over it. Boy, did that fox fight! But I got it back to The Animal House. The fox's owners said they didn't want to keep it any more. We called the city zoo, and they were happy to take the fox. Their fox had just died. We were lucky to find a home for that fox.

If it were up to me, though, there would be no zoos. An animal like a fox belongs in the open country where there are fields and brooks and hills.

But I'm glad there's a place like The Animal House. We do good things for animals, and I like working here.

The Stone Giant

A giant man of stone is found on Stub Newell's farm. How did it get there? Stub knows, but he's not tellng.

On a fall day in 1869, something very strange happened on Stub Newell's farm near the small town of Cardiff, New York. While digging a well, two men found a giant stone man under the ground. He was more than ten feet long!

Stub Newell had been out of town when the stone giant was found. When he came back, he found many people standing around the place where he had left the well diggers working. He walked over to see what everyone was looking at. He couldn't believe his eyes. The thing looked so real that it seemed as if it would get up and start walking around the farm.

Stub knew that something would be found on his farm. He just didn't know what it would be. A year before, George Hull, Stub's brother-in-law, had a very large box put in the ground on Stub's farm. At that time, George had told Stub to have someone accidentally find the box in a year. He thought it best that Stub be out of town when the box was found. George said that what was in the box would make them both a lot of money.

Now Stub knew what George had been talking about. Quickly, he put a sign up asking people to pay fifty cents to see the giant. People came from far and near. Stub was doing all right. Soon George came back. He took most of the money, but he gave Stub enough to keep him happy.

Stub was always afraid that someone would catch on, but nobody really did. Some, like Secretary Woolworth of the State University in Albany, thought that the giant was made from stone a long time ago. Others thought that the stone giant was a real man who had died ages ago. Why, the thing even had pores, very small holes, all over it! And Farmer Newell called attention to the giant's hand. He was holding it to himself as if he had been in pain at the time of his death.

An Onondaga Indian who lived near Stub's farm told of how giant Indians had once been at war with his people. His people made holes in the ground and covered them with leaves. Then they waited. If one of the giants fell into one of these holes, the Onondaga people covered him up and left him there. The Onondaga Indian thought that this is what happened to the stone giant.

Every day more and more people came to see the giant. Some came in wagons, others walked. Many took the train from New York City. As many as 3,000 people a day paid to see the giant. Soon Stub was asking them to pay a dollar to see the stone man. People didn't care. They still came.

But the money wasn't enough for George. So he thought about taking the giant on the road. He also thought about selling the giant to one of the many people who wanted to buy it. One of these was showman Phineas T. Barnum. He told George that he would pay $60,000 for the giant. When George said no, Barnum had his own stone man made. He called it the Cardiff Giant and showed it in New York City. George tried to stop Barnum, but he went right on showing the Cardiff Giant. Stories about the fight over the giant soon showed up in the papers. That's when people working for the papers made up their minds to find out where the giant came from once and for all.

What they finally found out was that George Hull had bought a very large piece of stone in Iowa. The stone had been shipped to Chicago. There a man had been paid to make a man out of stone, pores and all. People were found who said that they had seen the stone man on its way to New York State. The whole story was told in the papers for all to read.

Most people found the true story about the giant laughable. But Stub Newell didn't think it was so funny. He planned to leave his farm before the people from town could come to get him. But there was a surprise in store for Stub. No one was angry! People thought that he should get a medal for putting one over on the big city people. Why, people still came to see the giant. Stub and George made more money than before.

For years the giant stone man was shown at fairs. Today you can see him at the Farmer's Museum in Cooperstown, New York. Visitors are still surprised to see how real he looks.

Why They Run

Want to try a good sport that's easy to do and good for you? Try running.

All over, wherever you look, people are running. You may see men and women, older people and younger, out running along roads and streets. Where is everyone going? Nowhere, really. They're just running!

Running is a sport for everyone, everywhere. In cities, people will run for miles over city blocks, all the way across town and back again. In the country, people will run on and on, over green grass growing beside pretty roads.

If you're not a runner, you may wonder, "What's so much fun about running? What's so good about it? Don't you get tired? Don't your legs and feet hurt? What's the point of all that running?"

Of course, if you are a runner, you know the

answers to these questions. The most important thing is that running can be very good for your health. Your legs get much stronger within a few weeks after you start running. Your heart gets stronger too. Your heartbeat slows down, which is good. And you use oxygen better. Also, running is great for people who want to get thinner. It helps them burn up all the food they eat.

Most people run for better health. But many people run just for the fun of it. They like to see how far they can go.

Sometimes people do better than they ever thought they could. One woman started running in the spring. At first, she ran a mile a day. By early summer, she was up to four miles a day.

She kept on running almost every day. Now and then, she took a day off to rest. She grew healthier and stronger. One cool fall day, she tried to go more than four miles. It was a fine day for running. The air was clean. The trees were beautiful in their fall colors. She ran along country roads. Many-colored leaves fell all around her. She reached six miles that day, and she didn't even feel tired! Now, she hopes to run ten miles some day.

Sometimes, strange things happen to runners who are "working out" on roads and streets. Drivers in cars come close by and tease them. The drivers say things like, "Hey! Want a lift?" This isn't really funny, nor is it safe. When a runner is working hard, he or she needs good air, and not smoke from a passing car.

Many people like to run with **friends. They help** each other along, talking as they go. And more than one runner has found new friends while running. One man ran by himself every day in a city park. One day, another man started running beside him. The second man said, "You're running just fast enough for me. Do you mind if I run with you?"

"Not at all," the first man said, and they ran side by side for five miles. Since then, they've met every day to run together in the park.

People of all ages run. Not long ago, the newspapers had stories about an 87-year-old woman and a 101-year-old man. Both are runners! They don't go very fast, of course, but that isn't important. What is important is that they run. They both believe that running keeps them healthy.

If you would like to start running, there are some things you should know. First, you might want to see your doctor for a check-up. If you're not in good health, running could be the wrong thing to do. A lot of people have heart problems. Make sure that your heart is sound and strong before you start running. Running will make it even stronger.

Second, don't run too far at first. Your legs will get sore if you do. The first time you run, run for only a few minutes. The next day, go a little more. Each day, as you get stronger, you can go a little more.

Next, don't run too fast at first. It won't take long before you know how fast and how far you can go. Run easily, and go slowly at first. As you get to be a better runner, you'll find yourself running faster.

This is very important: Make sure you wear the right things on your feet. They should fit well and feel just right. If you run for many miles, your feet may start to hurt.

The best thing about running is that it's so easy to do. There's nothing to learn. You don't need any bats, balls, gloves, or anything else that you need for so many other sports. Just pick yourself up and run!

Nobody Knows You When You're Down and Out

All Gina needed was one lucky minute to change her from a has-been to a winner.

No one ever came right out and said, "Gina Rollins, you're finished!" They didn't have to. When a singer can't find a job after sixteen weeks, she knows she is finished.

It was three in the afternoon. Gina was still in her housecoat and her hair wasn't fixed. "You're a has-been," she told the face in her looking glass. "You're over the hill, lady. No more singing jobs for you!"

Even so, Gina kept hoping that someone would call to hire her. She had to earn some money. She couldn't even pay the rent, and it was almost the first of November.

Gina began singing in a low voice, "What have I got? Not one penny! And my friends? I haven't any!'' Gina couldn't get that old song out of her mind. What was the name of it? She couldn't remember.

Gina walked into the living room and turned on the TV. There was a new game show on called "Tune Times." Each player heard the first few notes of a song. Then he or she had to give the name of the song. If the player was right, a little bell would ring. Then the player could try to name more tunes and win more money. Gina moved closer to the TV set.

"This is easy!" she thought. "I could do better than that!" Then she thought, "Why not? Maybe I can get on the show!"

Gina reached for the phone. Then she put it down again. What if she tried and she lost? She would only feel worse than she did right now.

Gina finally called. She learned there was one opening on the show. It was on the first of November. When they told her she could be one of the players, Gina couldn't believe it. It was too good to be true.

On November first, Gina went to the TV station. She was on the air! And in a few minutes she had won the first two rounds! Gina knew she should take the money and run. But for the first time in a long time, she began to feel like a winner.

The MC looked at Gina. "This is it!" he told her. "Round three and a chance to win one hundred $100 bills! But if you're wrong, you get nothing! Are you sure you want to keep playing?"

Gina smiled and said, "You'd better believe it!"

In round three, Gina had to name three songs. The band played a few notes of the first one. "I know it," said Gina. "I know it . . . 'I've Got Plenty of Nothin'!'"

"Gina, you're right!" the MC yelled. "And you've got yourself twenty $100 bills! Want to quit?"

Gina couldn't stop now. "No! Never!" she said.

The next song was harder. Gina could remember some of the words. She sang to herself, "Since we're not together. . . ." What *was* the name? "Keeps raining all the time. . . ." Of course! "'Stormy Weather!'" Gina called out.

"You've got it, Gina, and you've also got fifty $100 bills. Do you want to keep on playing?"

"All the way!" Gina said. "I feel like a winner."

"Get ready!" cried the MC. "Get set. And tune in to *this*!"

The band played four notes and then four more. Gina closed her eyes. The words came back into her mind, "What have I got? Not one penny!" It was the old song she couldn't forget, with the name she couldn't remember!

The names of many old songs came into Gina's head, but she knew that none of them was right. Seconds flew by. Gina was ready to break down and cry. But then, out of nowhere, the answer came to her. "I've got it! It's 'Nobody Knows You When You're Down and Out.'"

"Oh, that's too bad!" the MC told her. "Too

bad, Gina!'' He looked at a little card. "No," he said, "the right answer is—"

"The right answer is the one I gave," Gina told him. "I'm sure of it."

The MC had his arm around her now. He was going to pull her away!

"I was singing that song on the day I called up to get on this show," Gina said, with tears in her eyes. "I have *lived* that song! Please listen!"

Right then and there Gina started singing! Then the band picked up the beat.

"When I get back on my feet again,
Then I'll meet my long-lost friends.
'It's mighty strange,' you can hear me shout.
'Nobody knows you when you're down and out!'
I mean: When you're down and out!"

When Gina finished, everyone was standing and calling for more. The MC made a sign for the camera to come in close.

"Gina Rollins," he said in his most important voice, "you were right! I was looking at the wrong answer card. That means that you win . . . one hundred $100 bills!"

When the clapping died down, he asked: "Gina, what are you going to do with all that money?"

Gina smiled right at the camera. "Now that I know I can be a winner," she said, "I'm going to keep right on singing. What else?"

ADI STRONG HAND
and the Indian Way

This is based on the true story of an American Indian family and some very hard times in their lives.

"I want to get a job because we need the money," said Adi Strong Hand to her husband, Don.

Don was angry. "My mother and her mother and *her* mother always stayed at home. It is the Indian way," Don said firmly. He was a Sioux and proud of it. Adi did not like to fight, so she said no more.

It was 11:30 at night, five weeks later, when Adi awakened her husband. Their youngest child, Steve, had been sick for three days and had suddenly taken a turn for the worse. His body was very hot.

"You had better go get the medicine man," Adi told Don. He was tired, but he got out of bed and dressed quickly. Then he went out into the cold, South Dakota night. He jumped into his old car and rode down the highway toward the village where the medicine man lived.

Suddenly, Don saw a police car behind him with its bright red light. "What do they want this time?" he thought. "I don't have time to stop." The police car came up beside Don.

"Pull over!" the policeman yelled. Don slowed down.

"Stop!" the policeman yelled angrily. "Your car makes too much noise. You need a new tail pipe."

Don yelled back, "I can't stop now—my son is sick!" He stepped on the gas. A second later, a gunshot broke across the night. Don's car turned, ran into a snow bank, and stopped dead.

Don woke up in the hospital. A bullet had hit him in the back and stuck there. He tried to move his foot, but he couldn't. He couldn't feel his feet or his legs.

Then he saw his wife, Adi, at his bedside. Her eyes were filled with tears. "The doctors say you won't be able to walk again," she said quietly.

Don's face fell. "No," he said. "It can't be true!"

But Adi could see the pain and fear that Don was feeling. She could see that Don knew it *was* true.

"You'll be able to get around in a wheelchair," said Adi. "And there are ways you can still work."

"But I'll never walk again!" Don cried. "I'll never walk again, and only because my car had a broken tail pipe!"

In his anger Don had forgotten to ask about his son. Suddenly he remembered. "How is Steve?"

"He's all right," said Adi. "He's getting better."

Don was in the hospital for seven weeks. While he was there, he and Adi made plans for a new life. Although Don had said that it was the Indian way for a woman to stay at home, Adi knew that now she had to work. They would leave South Dakota and move back to Adi's home in New Mexico. There, in the Pueblo Indian country where she had grown up, Adi would make a living for them and their three children.

At lunch one day, Adi told Don she had started working at the government Indian office near her village in New Mexico.

"Why do you want to work for them?" Don said. "You know they are against Indians."

"They are changing. I can make them change more," Adi said. "You'll see. I'll help them understand Indian problems better."

The Indians of New Mexico were not used to the ways of the white world, and yet they had to live in it. Adi's job was to help them learn how to live in it. Many Indian women needed to earn money to help their families. Adi held classes to teach them how to look for jobs.

Adi also helped white doctors understand that many Indians still believed only in treatment by medicine men. Soon, government doctors began to let Indian medicine men treat some people in hospitals.

Adi began to love her work, but Don was feeling the sameness of each day in his wheelchair. Without a job, his life seemed empty. Don did a lot of thinking about how to make his life more useful. He finally told Adi, "I'd like to visit my Dad's farm back in South Dakota."

At his father's, Don wheeled himself around the small farm. He talked to people who wanted to buy cows. He began to feel good again.

After that, Don decided to go for a few months each year to work with his Dad. Now Don had a job too. One day, Adi telephoned him at the farm with good news. "We've won! The government is paying us $50,000 because the policeman shot you," she said. They knew that no money could give Don back what he had lost. But it was a help.

Through these troubled times Adi kept her family together. Their new life was working. And little by little, Adi was helping white people understand the Indian way.

If your head feels pushed in tight, your eyes are almost shut, you smell something funny, and one foot is cold, don't worry. You most likely have your sock pulled over your head!

A Stranger Comes to Town
Part 1

In a town where nothing much happens, it's a big day when a stranger gets off the train. And when the stranger is a beautiful woman, it's an even bigger day.

In the winter, the train came to our town just once a week. We could always hear it coming a long way off. Some people said you could hear it twelve miles away on a good day. It would come blowing and choking around the last hill, beat its way past all the snow, and finally jar to a stop at the little station.

We boys would all come down to meet it. You've got to understand, nothing much ever happened in our town, so the train coming in was a big thing. It would stay for only a minute or two. We would look in the windows to see if anyone was riding the train, and ask them where they were going. A man would drop off a bag of mail, and pick up another. One or two boxes would come off the train, one or two would go on. Then the stationman would shout

down the track to the engineer, "OK, let her go."
And the train would slowly start its long pull out of
town.

That was it. No one ever got on or off. Not in the
winter. Never in the winter. Well, that's not really
true. Once, a long time ago, someone got off. And it
was deep in the dead of winter. A long time ago.

This is where my story really starts.

I was 18. The town was starting to get a little
"small" for me, if you know what I mean. I wasn't
doing much, just a little work for my father. Besides
that, there wasn't anything to do, and I was getting
restless.

It was a bad winter. But every week we boys went
down to the station to wait for the train. Like I said,
there was nothing else to do.

It was the coldest day of the year. Snow blew up
and down the track as we waited for the train to get
in. I was hopping around, trying to keep a little heat
moving into my feet. My hands were deep in my
pockets. It was cold! I was starting to be sorry I had
come to wait for the train.

The train came in a little late. "Snow on the
tracks," the engineer called to the man in the ticket
window. Gray smoke filled the air around us as the
train stood in the station. The mail was picked up,
the mail was dropped off. Just like always.

But then a door opened in one of the cars. One of
the trainmen hopped down, and he set up some stairs
for someone to get off the train. We all went to look.
A woman came to the top stair. She was about 30,

maybe, though I wasn't sure. She was wearing a long, brown coat and a matching hat. But the main thing I saw was her eyes. They were black, shining black, like the winter night. I had never seen such a beautiful woman in my whole life.

She came down the stairs. The trainman put two bags down beside her. The cold didn't seem to bother her. She stood there for a minute, and then she looked right at me. "Young man," she said, "would you please help me with my bags?"

"Yes, ma'am," I said, and I ran up and got a hold of them. Some other boys ran up too, but she didn't pay any attention to them. She just looked at me and said, "You take one. I'll take the other." Then she turned and set off, and I followed her down the wide main street of the town.

She knew just where to go, which was strange, because none of us had ever seen her in the town before. She went right to Mrs. Newton's boarding house, where she took a room.

She thanked me for helping her, and then she asked me my name. "Steven," I said. Then she reached into her pocketbook. I knew she wanted to give me some money for helping her.

"That's OK," I said. "Glad to help."

She looked at me for a second with those black, black eyes. Then she smiled and closed her pocketbook. "Steven," she said, "you've got class."

I had made a friend.

Weeks passed. They were cold weeks. But for me

they were new and wonderful. Because two or three times each week, the black-eyed woman would ask me to have lunch with her. I always said yes.

She asked me questions. I told her about myself, about the town, about the country thereabouts. I told her a lot, and she listened very carefully. She never got tired of listening. I didn't think that anyone from outside could care so much about the town. As I said before, nothing much ever happened there.

My friends would get on me. "Hey, Steven. Who is she? What does she want here?" I didn't know so I didn't say. All I knew was that she was a real nice woman. A real nice, beautiful woman.

End of Part 1

A Stranger Comes to Town

Part 2

When the strange woman leaves town, she leaves some of her thoughts with Steven.

The winter stayed on. Snow kept falling, and the cold never broke. It held on tight, closing around our very bones. No one could remember a worse winter. But every week, in wind and storm, the boys would go to the station to wait for the train. Just like always. We'd all stand there, the train would come and go, and then we'd go back to our cold, little homes.

Yet for me it was a good time. Each week I would wait for the black-eyed woman to ask me to lunch. She always did. We talked and talked.

At other times I would see her in town. She went around to the stores. She was friendly, and she talked with a lot of people. Everyone seemed to like her, but some of the older people looked down when she walked by.

I still didn't know why she had come to our town.

One day my father called me into the kitchen. "Sit down, Steven," he said. He didn't look straight at me when he talked. He kind of looked away. "Son, I know you're almost a man."

"Yes, Dad."

"Almost, but not yet."

"Yes, Dad."

"Son," and now he looked down at his hands, "I want to know, just what is it you and that woman talk about?"

"Nothing, Dad. I just talk about myself."

"Son . . . I know you're a good boy. I want you to tell me true. . . ."

"I told you, Dad. We just sit and we talk!" I stood up and looked hard at him. "Is that all, Dad?"

My father didn't seem to know what to say. I started to walk out of the kitchen, but I turned and looked back at my father. He was still sitting there, real quiet. And I said, this time in a low voice, "I don't know who she is, Dad. But something tells me you do." He didn't answer, and I left.

Finally, the winter began to die.

One clear night I was out walking alone in the snow. In the sky the stars looked on coldly. But I could tell that winter was ending. I could feel the change. The deep, dark space above me seemed to fill me with gladness. I felt as light as a balloon, and just as ready to take off and fly! "I wish I could," I thought. "I wish I could."

Near me then, I heard a voice. "Hello, Steven." I

turned. It was the black-eyed woman. She, too, was out walking in the snow.

"Hello," I answered.

"Steven," she said, "I'm leaving this town. Soon."

"Leaving?" I said. My heart sank like a rock in a pond. "But it's almost spring. It's beautiful here in the spring."

"I know."

"How do you know? You've never been here in the spring!"

"Yes, I have, Steven. Yes, I have." She looked up. "What a lovely night," she said. Then she turned to me. "Steven, you've been a good friend to me. But I've never told you anything about myself. Now I will."

She smiled, sadly it seemed. "I used to live here," she said, "when I was . . . younger."

"You did?"

"I was just a girl." She stopped talking for a second, and then she went on. "You might say I got into a bit of trouble. I really didn't do anything wrong. What happened isn't important now. But the people of this town made me feel worthless and bad. So I left. I was just a girl."

I looked at her closely. "Why did you come back?" I said.

"Just to see if things have changed."

"Have they?" I asked.

"Well," she said, "most of the people have been real good to me. They've changed. But I've changed too. I've learned. . . ."

"Yes?"

"I've learned that a person often has to go away to grow up. But sooner or later, you have to come back to find out who you are."

Two days later she was gone. When the train came in, she got on and rode away. But everyone else stayed.

My friends were quiet with me after that. They didn't ask me about the black-eyed woman. My father didn't talk to me much. I sat around a lot, looking off toward the hills.

Winter ended, and spring came. In a month or so, the train was coming in every two days again. With the snow gone, the tracks were always open.

"Steve!" a friend called to me one day. "There's a new train on the line! A beauty! It's called the *Rocket*! Do you want to see it? Come on!"

"No, thanks!" I called back. "Some other time."

But I *did* see the *Rocket* come in that day. It came in like a silver wind, raising dust and storming around the hill into our little town. And while the boys watched and waved as the *Rocket* left town, none of them saw me leaving too, sitting in the very last car, watching my little town slip slowly away into the past.

So many things look good at the supermarket. How can we find the best buys for our money—and for our health?

A QUESTION OF FOOD

Some people say we're pretty lucky when it comes to food. After all, we've got more kinds of food than people in other countries. Our supermarkets carry over 10,000 foods! So we can take our pick from the many boxes, cans, jars, trays, and bags on the shelves. We can hunt around the store until we spot just what we want.

We've got lots of "convenience" foods too. These are foods that are easy to cook. We can buy a frozen food, put it in the oven, and have a full course supper in no time. We can open a can of soup and warm it on the stove in a few minutes, while homemade soup takes hours. We can even eat foods that we don't know how to cook, because food companies do it for us. Everything is made so easy.

It seems too good to be true.

Maybe it is too good to be true. Some people think that our food picture isn't really all that bright. Eating a lot of food doesn't mean we eat the right foods. And it's not that easy to pick from all those foods.

Before you buy food, you should ask yourself a lot of questions:

WHAT FOODS ARE BEST FOR YOUR BODY? "Junk foods" are foods that don't do you any good. They may fill you up, but they don't help young people grow or keep older people in good health. People who eat a lot of junk food probably get sick more often than people who eat good food.

Because the government now makes food companies tell what goes into their goods, it's important to read labels. In this way, you can find out what's in the food. You can also find out if it's good for you.

FRESH OR FROZEN? This is an important question because it has to do with what you pay for food. Sometimes, frozen foods cost more. But they also save time. That brings us to another question:

WILL YOU MAKE IT YOURSELF OR LET A FOOD COMPANY DO IT FOR YOU? Whenever you buy food that saves time, you probably pay more for the convenience. If you buy a frozen supper, it will probably cost more than if you had bought fresh food and made your supper yourself.

But some convenience foods don't cost more. So the best way to find out for sure is to add it all up.

When you're thinking about buying a convenience food, read the label. Then think of what it would cost to put the same things together yourself. Sometimes you may pick the convenience food and other times you may make it yourself. The important thing is to think about it.

When it comes to "doing it yourself," you may even want to grow some of your own food, not buy it. Planting seeds doesn't take much time. And it's fun to eat what you grew yourself.

WHAT SIZE DO YOU BUY? That's a hard question to answer when you think about how many sizes there are in the supermarket. How do you know which one is the best buy? You must think about the supermarket's price and how many people you're buying for. Bigger sizes often cost less. But if your family can't finish a food before it spoils, you probably should have picked a smaller size.

HOW WILL YOU KNOW IF THE FOOD IS FRESH? Some food, like milk, is dated, so you know if it is fresh or about to spoil. It's too bad that more foods don't have dates. Many people believe that food in cans or boxes can't spoil. That's not true. No food can stay fresh on the shelf forever. Some foods stay fresh longer than others. But after a while on the shelf, all foods go bad.

DO YOU KNOW HOW TO STORE FOOD? When you bring food home, it's up to you to keep it from spoiling. Frozen foods belong in the freezer until you're ready to use them. With frozen meat, once you let it unfreeze, you shouldn't put it back into the freezer again. You can keep some canned foods up to a year, but most canned foods should be used before that time.

That's a lot of questions to think about. You might even have a big frown on your face the next time you go food shopping. But it pays off in the end. Eating is one of the most important things you do. So you might as well do it right!

A gunman came out of a show one day, pushed his gun in the ticket window, and said, "I didn't like the show. Give me everyone's money back!"

A FABLE

A father doesn't want his eleven sons fighting with one another. So he thinks of a plan to make them get along.

Once there was a farmer who had eleven sons. The oldest son was thirty, and the youngest was sixteen. All of the sons worked on the farm.

Now the farmer loved his sons, and the eleven sons loved their father. But the sons did not get along well together. They would shout at one another and yell and fight and get nothing done. The farmer couldn't understand it.

"Why do brothers fight so much?" he asked a friend one day.

"The wolf and the dog are brothers, too," the friend answered. "There is no reason why brothers fight. They just fight."

The farmer owned a large farm where he raised corn. His cornfields reached for miles and miles.

But the farmer was growing old. He often felt tired, and he began to wonder how his sons would get along if he should die.

So one summer day the farmer called all his sons together on the porch. In the fields, golden ears of corn were growing. The farmer looked out at the fields, and then he looked at his sons. "When I die," he said, "you young men will have to take care of the farm. Can you do it without me?"

The eleven sons said nothing. Some just stood with their hands in their pockets. Others folded their arms and looked away. So the farmer went on talking.

"This farm will belong to all of you when I die," he said. "There will be plenty for all of you. But if you go on fighting, and working against one another, I don't see how you can work these large cornfields. You won't be able to do all the things that must be done on this big farm."

The sons listened, but they didn't hear. Sad to say, they kept right on fighting just as they always had.

The farmer watched his sons, and he tried to think of a way to help them. And finally, he had a plan which seemed like it might work. He hoped it would teach them something.

One afternoon, he sent for all his sons. They stood by him as he spoke. "Boys, I am feeling worse every day," he told them. "But there is something you could do to please me."

The sons listened.

"Go out to the forest," the farmer told them,

"and each of you bring me two thin sticks."

The sons thought this was a strange thing for their father to ask. They could not think of any reason for him to ask for sticks. But they could see that he was worse. He was dying. So they made up their minds to do as he asked.

The sons went to the forest, and each one brought back to his father two thin sticks.

"Thank you," said the farmer. From each son, he took just one stick. The farmer was tired, but he knew he had to do this. He put the eleven sticks together and he tied them with a rope.

"There!" said the farmer. "Now," he said, "each of you hold up the stick you have left." Each son held up his one stick.

"Break it!" the farmer said. And each son broke his stick in half.

"Very good!" said the farmer. "Each of you broke one stick!"

Now the farmer held up the eleven sticks he had tied together. "These eleven sticks are like my eleven sons. Try to break them, now that they are tied together!"

Each son tried to break the eleven sticks that were tied together. No one could do it. The eleven sticks together were too strong.

The farmer looked at his sons and said, "Eleven sticks apart can be broken easily. But eleven sticks TOGETHER cannot be broken! Eleven sticks together are strong! And eleven brothers who stick together will always be strong!"

From that day on, the farmer knew, his sons would always stick together.

Mr. Brown was a very rich man, but he never gave a penny to anyone. One day someone asked him, "How come you never give any money to help other people?"

Mr. Brown answered, "First of all, I have a sister who lost her husband, and she has six children. Do you know how much it costs to help a family like that? Then, my father is 97, my mother is 95, and they have doctor bills that are hard to believe. Well, I don't give money to any of them, so why should I give it to anyone else?"

Last of the Small-Time Fishermen

**Pablo and Miguel know one life—
the life of a fisherman.**

Mallorca ("Ma-*yor*-kah") is an island that sits in the sea, one hundred miles from Spain. It is a warm and beautiful island. Its people live quiet lives, but many of them must work hard to make a living.

Miguel and his brother Pablo live in a small village on the north side of Mallorca. Their faces are lined from years of working in the sun. They are fishermen. All the men in their family have always been fishermen. For these "small-time fishermen," things haven't changed much over the years. The two brothers still work in much the same way that their father's father did.

For most of each year, Miguel and Pablo live in a boathouse by the shore. The brothers go out to sea every day when the weather isn't too stormy. They go to the fishing grounds and cast out their nets. This is easy work, and the two men take their time at it.

The next morning, well before the sun comes up, they go out again to pull up the nets. Now the work is harder. Miguel stands at one end of the boat and pulls in the nets. Pablo sits behind him and puts the fish into a large basket. The men work without talking. They must work with speed. If they can get back to the village before the other fishermen do, they have a better chance of selling their whole catch.

By the time the sun comes up, Miguel and Pablo have finished their job. The brothers hurry back to their boathouse, hoping to beat the other fishermen to the shore. Pablo then sets out toward the village, carrying the basket full of fish on his back. Miguel stays behind to clean out their boat and to tie the nets up to dry in the morning sun.

Pablo almost always reaches the village before the town hall clock strikes eight. He is often the first fisherman to get there. He stands in the middle of the main street, cups his hands around his mouth, and yells out, "Fresh fish! Fresh fish! *Pescado fresco!*"

Doors open on both sides of the street. Women come out of their homes with bags or large dishes in their hands. They stand in a ring around Pablo, and bargain with him over the price of his fish.

"How much do you want for this one?" asks one older woman. She touches a big brown fish.

"50 *pesetas*."

"I'll give you 30," says the woman.

Pablo says, "This fish is too nice for 30. Make it 45."

She says, "40."

"Sold!" says Pablo.

When Pablo has finished selling to these women, he moves on to the village's smaller streets. By the end of the morning, he has gone around the whole town. On many days, he can sell all his fish. But sometimes he has fish left over. When this happens, he has to sell what is left at a very low price, or he gives it to the village cats.

Meanwhile, at the boathouse, Miguel is mending any nets which have been broken by big fish. In the afternoon, Pablo comes back to help him. When the brothers have finished with their mending, they go out in the boat to cast the nets again. This goes on day after day. Fishing, like most other work, is a job that never changes and never ends.

Until a few years ago, the people of this village didn't have much money. They couldn't buy meat more than one or two times a month. Fish was one of their most important foods, so fishermen like Miguel and Pablo made a good living.

But times have changed. The people have better jobs now, and they make more money than they used to. They eat meat every day, and they buy fish only when they feel like it. Miguel and Pablo are not happy about this, of course. They now have a hard time getting by.

But the brothers won't have to worry about this problem much longer. They are getting on in years, and they have no children. When they get too old to go out to sea anymore, they will try to sell their boat and their boathouse. Then they will go to live out their lives in their house in the village.

For now, however, Miguel and Pablo will keep on fishing. They have been fishermen all their lives, and they are set in their ways. They don't know how to do anything else, nor would they want to do anything else.

"I love the sea," says Miguel, "and I love my work. I will never stop doing it." As he says this, Pablo looks on sadly and nods.

Jim: I'm having a lot of trouble with my tooth. It has been hurting a lot lately.
Jack: If it were my tooth, I'd have it taken out.
Jim: If it were yours, I would, too.

Return from the Deep

Paula reached out to her husband from a deep sleep. Is this what saved his life?

Dr. Benson's touch was quick and gentle as he started to dig the last splinters of glass from Paula's arms and chest. Dr. Robbins worked next to him, washing out the deep cuts and closing them with her sure hands.

Paula and her husband, Ray, had been in a car crash that afternoon. Ray was near death when they got to the hospital. For five hours, two doctors had done their best to save his life. Now, he might live and he might die. The only thing anyone could do now was wait.

At first, Paula's cuts did not seem that bad. Now, Dr. Benson wasn't so sure. "She's starting to bleed inside," Dr. Benson said. "There must be more splinters. If I'm right they're just above the heart

117

where we can't see them.''

"Then we'll have to go inside," Dr. Robbins told him. "We can't borrow any more time for her. We can't afford to wait any longer."

Paula had been given sleeping gas, of course. But something strange was happening. She could hear the two doctors talking. She couldn't really make out what they were saying, but she could feel how worried the voices were. They worried about something near her heart. They worried about someone else, too.

Paula couldn't speak. But she found that she could open her eyes. How strange! A man and a woman were standing together. They seemed to be covered with bright, beautiful lights.

"Be careful," Dr. Robbins said. "She's almost awake!"

"She's a real fighter," Dr. Benson said. "I'll put her under again and keep her there."

Paula heard their voices getting softer as the gas mask put her into a deeper sleep. She dropped down past soft clouds. Down and down she went.

In her sleep, Paula saw a beautiful, brown-eyed man. White clouds seemed to cover his face. A voice in her mind seemed to say, "Do you take this man? Do you take each other as husband and wife?"

Paula wanted so much to be the bride of the beautiful man. She knew him from somewhere. But he seemed to be in trouble. He was drowning in the sea. The sea was the color of blood.

Now, in her mind, Paula heard the voice again,

"For better or worse, in sickness and in health, until death do you part."

She must save him! She must get him back to dry land! In her mind, Paula reached out and held the man. Suddenly, she knew who he was. He was Ray, her husband. Was this really happening? Paula felt herself growing tired. It was too hard to keep Ray and herself above the waters. The waters turned cold. She must stay with Ray. Only death could keep them apart. Was she dying now? Was Ray? He seemed to say, "It's useless, Paula! Goodbye!"

In another room of the hospital, a doctor looked at Ray and said, "He seems worse. He may not live."

In her deep sleep, Paula kept fighting. She pulled Ray from the waters. She made a fire out of shining, silver pieces of wood. The flames flew up like shooting stars. Paula pulled Ray inside the fire with her. It did not burn. It covered them with flames. The fire seemed to be growing right inside them. It made soft lights dance in the air. Slowly the lights changed into morning sunshine.

A doctor looked at Ray. "He's going to make it! He's going to live!"

It was morning. Dr. Benson and Dr. Robbins found Paula awake when they walked into her room. She was watching the sunshine as it danced in her window and fell onto the covers of her bed. Paula heard their steps and turned to look at the doctors. She pointed at them. "I know you both," she said. "You saved my life."

"No, we didn't," Dr. Robbins said. "All we did

was clean your cuts and close them up. You did the rest. You found a reason for living and you held on to life.''

"The reason was Ray," Paula said. "I knew he was in trouble so I went looking for him to save him. I know he's OK. I was with him all night."

The doctors looked at each other. What was she talking about? And how could she be so sure that her husband was alive?

Paula could tell they didn't understand what she was trying to say. "I found Ray under the sea," she said. "He was drowning."

"What sea?" Dr. Benson asked.

"The sea of blood," Paula said. "Maybe it was the sea of death."

The doctors didn't know what to say. "You need rest," Dr. Robbins said. "We'll be leaving now."

Did it really happen, or was it all in her mind? For one second, as the sunlight spilled into the room, Paula knew the answer. She had gone over to another place, another world. And she had returned, bringing Ray back with her.

Both doctors talked about Paula as they left her room. "Her mind is troubled," Dr. Benson said. "She's had a hard fight. She doesn't know what she's saying."

"Still, her husband was just about gone," Dr. Robbins said. "He'd lost the will to live. But somehow, he found it again."

"You can't explain something like that," Dr. Benson said. "Sometimes, it just happens."

In her room, Paula rested in the sunlight, knowing that she and Ray would soon be together again.

Write the name Sam or Joe for each blank.

1. _____ wasn't happy about the money he lost.
2. _____ was well dressed.
3. _____ came into Ned's Place for the first time.
4. _____ was new in Yuko City.
5. _____ was going to blow up because he was getting bad cards.

Show the order in which these events happened in the story by writing 1, 2, 3, 4, and 5.

6. _____ Sam walked over to Joe's table and sat down.
7. _____ The gun went off in Joe's hand.
8. _____ Sam came into Ned's Place.
9. _____ Someone gave Sam a gun.
10. _____ Sam told Joe that Joe was cheating.

Find the one correct answer.

11. _____ This story happened about
   a. 200 years ago.
   b. 80 years ago.
   c. 10 years ago.
12. _____ Sam Dasher
   a. played cards for a living.
   b. worked in a warehouse.
   c. worked in a bank.
13. _____ Bad Joe
   a. liked winning at cards.
   b. never cheated at cards.
   c. didn't play cards.

14. _____ Sam Dasher
    a. was fast with a gun.
    b. was new at shooting guns.
    c. had his own gun.

15. _____ Another good name for this story is
    a. "Bad Day for Bad Joe."
    b. "Sam Dasher Plays Cards."
    c. "People in Yuko City Help Out."

Check on page 162

BA-2 ━━━━━━━━ OLD SILVER, OLD GOLD

Show the order in which these events happened in the story by writing 1, 2, 3, 4, and 5.

1. _____ One of them had to stay on the boat to watch the gold and silver.
2. _____ Bill came up with two pieces of gold.
3. _____ They began to run out of gas and food.
4. _____ Another boat came to the spot.
5. _____ Bill was on the sea floor nearly an hour.

Write T if the sentence is True, F if it is False, and ? if the story doesn't tell.

6. _____ The ship went down 40 years ago.
7. _____ Bill saw the old ship when he went down.
8. _____ It had gone down about ten miles from shore.
9. _____ Others did find gold and silver there years ago.
10. _____ Word gets around fast when someone is looking for gold.

11. _____ Bill and Alice made their living finding gold.
12. _____ Bill and Alice looked for over three weeks.
13. _____ They don't think that they will be back to look for more silver and gold.
14. _____ The people on the other boat didn't find anything.

Find the one correct answer.

15. _____ This story is about
    a. two people who are looking for gold and silver under water.
    b. how to find gold and silver in the sand.
    c. a ship that had gone down in a storm with a million dollars on board.

Check on page 162

BA-3 ▬▬▬▬▬▬▬▬ THE CATCH OF TIME

Write **T** if the sentence is True. Write **PT** if the sentence tells what some people **think** is true.

1. _____ "Well, it is a dirty book."
2. _____ "They shouldn't give you that book in school!"
3. _____ There was a big fight going on in the city of Stanton.
4. _____ Mr. Sitwell called a meeting of some of his friends.
5. _____ Many young people read *The Catch of Time* to find the dirty parts.

6. _____ "It is poisoning our children's minds."
7. _____ David's parents didn't want him to read the book.
8. _____ "It is a good book and our children should read it."

Find the one correct answer.

9. _____ The teacher was telling the children that they
   a. shouldn't do as their parents told them.
   b. must make up their own minds on right and wrong.
   c. must read only the books the teacher told them to read.

10. _____ A good new name for this story could be
   a. "Marla and David."
   b. "A Dirty Book."
   c. "To Read or Not to Read."

Check on page 162

BA-4 ▬▬▬▬ GOING BACK TO SCHOOL

Show the order in which these events happened in the story by writing, 1, 2, 3, 4, and 5.

1. ___ Mrs. Wilson told Mary it was time to grow up.
2. ___ Mary told Mrs. Wilson she was going to night school.
3. ___ Mary was reading the want ads.
4. ___ Mary headed toward the school.
5. ___ Mary's father told her he was happy she was going back to school.

Write <u>T</u> if the sentence is True. <u>F</u> if it is False, and <u>?</u> if the story doesn't tell.

6. ___ Mary lives with her father and brother.

7. ___ Mary dropped out of school four years ago.

8. ___ Mrs. Wilson was friends with Mary's mother.

9. ___ Mary doesn't care what Mrs. Wilson thinks of her.

10. ___ Mary's father works in a store.

11. ___ Mary likes to take walks in the morning.

12. ___ Mrs. Wilson is a cleaning woman.

13. ___ Mary found a good job after she dropped out of school.

14. ___ Mrs. Wilson doesn't want Mary to go to night school.

Find the one correct answer.

15. ___ A good new name for this story could be
   a. "Growing Up."
   b. "Mrs. Wilson's Children."
   c. "Looking for Work."

Check on page 162

Find the correct ending for each sentence.

1. _____ At first Bonnie
       told Ms. Lewis
2. _____ Fifi told Bonnie
3. _____ Helen told
       Bonnie
4. _____ Bonnie was angry

a. that she didn't
   say what she
   thought.
b. what she wanted
   to hear.
c. that the wood had
   a spell on it.
d. she wanted to eat
   at the Gold
   Sword.

Show the order in which these events happened in the story by writing 1, 2, 3, 4, and 5.

5. _____ Bonnie thinks it is time to see Fifi.
6. _____ Bonnie is angry with herself for not telling
       Ms. Lewis what she thinks.
7. _____ Bonnie finds out she has helped herself.
8. _____ Bonnie tells Helen it's OK to change eating
       places.
9. _____ Bonnie thinks the piece of wood has helped
       her.

Find the one correct answer.

10. _____ This story is about a woman who
    a. likes to play jokes on people.
    b. likes to eat out a lot.
    c. learns to believe in herself.

Check on page 163

128

Find the correct ending for each sentence.

_____ 1. Blood is needed	a. to make blood.
_____ 2. There is no way	b. to give blood.
_____ 3. It takes a little time	c. to keep blood cold.
_____ 4. The blood you give goes	d. to a blood bank.
	e. to help save lives.
_____ 5. The blood bank is the place	

Write T if the sentence is True, F if it is False, and ? if the story doesn't tell.

_____ 6. Some blood banks wouldn't take Dr. Drew's blood.

_____ 7. Blood can be stored in blood banks for many years.

_____ 8. Black people can give blood only to other black people.

_____ 9. There are only two kinds of blood.

_____ 10. Your doctor must know what kind of blood you have before blood is given to you.

_____ 11. You must be over 17 to give blood.

_____ 12. You can give blood even if you are sick.

_____ 13. The kind of blood that is the hardest to find is B.

_____ 14. Most people know what kind of blood they have.

Find the one correct answer.

15. _____ This story is mainly about
   a. why giving blood is important and what happens to the blood after it is given.
   b. how you can tell if you have A, B, AB, or O blood.
   c. why it is hard to store blood and how the stored blood gets to the people who need it.

Check on page 163

BA-7 ANGELA, RAY, AND CLOUDY DAY

Read each sentence. Read the names in the box. Find the two names that go in each sentence. Some names will be used more than once.

Angela	Ray	Mr. Homes	Cloudy Day

A. (1) _____ said, "I want you to ride Cloudy Day in the race" to (2) _____.

B. (3) _____ said, "You've got to win" to (4) _____.

C. (5) _____ said, "I wonder why I never saw you before" to (6) _____.

D. (7) _____ said, "I don't think I'll be able to go out with all of you tonight" to (8) _____.

Show the order in which these events happened in the story by writing 1, 2, 3, 4, and 5.

9. _____ Ray gets to ride Cloudy Day in the race.

10. _____ Ray gets a job taking care of Cloudy Day.

11. _____ Ray thinks Angela isn't his kind of girl after all.

12. _____ When Ray wins the race, Angela ''sees'' him.

13. _____ Cloudy Day's rider gets sick.

Find the one correct answer.

14. _____ Ray thought Angela liked him only because

    a. she was little, too.

    b. he had won the race.

    c. he was a kind man.

15. _____ This story is about

    a. Ray's winning the race even though he was not a good rider.

    b. Ray's wanting Angela to like him for winning the race.

    c. Ray's finding out he is too <u>big</u> a person for Angela.

Check on page 163

Read each sentence. Read the words in the box. Find the word that goes in each sentence.

good	loved	56	think

1. Will was _____ years old when he died.
2. People all over knew and _____ Will Rogers.
3. He wanted to make people laugh, but he wanted them to _____ too.
4. When a man talked about himself, Will said he never heard anything but _____.

What kind of man was Will Rogers? Write T for all the true statements and write F for all the false statements.

5. _____ He cared only about money.
6. _____ He would be fun to know.
7. _____ He loved people.
8. _____ He was true to himself and what he believed.
9. _____ He couldn't take a joke.
10. _____ He wanted to do rope tricks all the time.
11. _____ He wanted people to think about important things.
12. _____ He thought going to war made the country strong.
13. _____ He never forgot what it is like to be without money.
14. _____ He liked to tell stories about Indians killing cowboys.

Find the one correct answer.

15. ____ A good new name for this story could be
   a. "A Man to Remember."
   b. "A Proud Indian."
   c. "The Wild West Show."

Check on page 163

BA-9━━━━━━━━━**READ ALL ABOUT IT**

Find the correct ending for each sentence.

1. ____ After Joe hurt his hand,
2. ____ After Joe read about beating the Wheels,
3. ____ After Joe read about hurting his hand,
4. ____ After Joe believed there was a spell on the paper,

a. the Cats beat the Wheels.
b. he caught his hand in the door.
c. he planned to make millions.
d. the spell was over.

When did things happen in the story? Show it by writing 1, 2, 3, 4, and 5.

5. ____ Joe reads about Al Wood's hit in the paper.
6. ____ Joe reads about his hand being hurt.
7. ____ Joe reads that Blake's home run won the game for the Cats.
8. ____ Al Wood's hit wins the game for the Cats.
9. ____ Willie Blake makes a home run.

Find the one correct answer.

10. _____ A good new name for this story could be
   a. "Blake's Home Run."
   b. "Joe Bats Out."
   c. "The Strange Newspaper."

Check on page 164

BA-10■■■■■■■■■■■■■■■■■■■**THE RACE:**
A FABLE FOR OUR TIME

Write one of the words from the box to complete each sentence below. Use each word only once.

| back | winner | chicken | got | man | run |

The man Pat was to marry was to be picked this way:
All the men had to 1. _____ around the lake. Then they
2. _____ an egg at Mr. Clay's 3. _____ house. After
that, they ran 4. _____ to the lake. The first 5. _____
to come back was the 6. _____ .

Find the correct ending for each sentence.

7. _____ The fastest runner
8. _____ Pat had six weeks
9. _____ Pat looked like a man
10. _____ Winning the race

a. was very important to Pat.
b. in her brother's clothes.
c. to become the fastest runner.
d. would marry Pat.

Check on page 164

BA-11 ▬▬▬▬▬SOMEONE ELSE'S WATCH

Find the correct ending for each sentence.

1. _____ Cerita picked up
2. _____ At first, she made up her mind
3. _____ Cerita could hear
4. _____ She thought people knew
5. _____ Cerita took the watch to work
6. _____ The owner was happy

a. the watch wasn't hers.
b. to find the owner.
c. to have the watch again.
d. a beautiful gold watch.
e. the ticking get louder.
f. to keep the watch.

Write T if the sentence is True, F if it is False, and ? if the story doesn't tell.

7. _____ Cerita was sure that it would be easy to find the owner of the watch.

8. _____ Cerita didn't like the way the watch looked on her.

9. _____ Cerita had a lot of fun wearing the watch.

10. _____ Cerita liked showing off the watch in stores.

11. _____ The watch seemed to tick louder and louder.

12. _____ The watch cost over $200.

13. _____ The woman gave Cerita some money for finding her watch.

14. _____ Deep inside her, Cerita knew she could never keep the watch.

Find the one correct answer.

15. _____ This story is about Cerita, who learned that

a. it was no fun worrying about a watch she had found.

b. finders are keepers.

c. a gold watch doesn't have to cost a lot of money.

Check on page 164

Write one of the words from the box to complete each sentence below.

| life | Americans | earth | craters | sun |

1. When the _____ shines on part of the moon, that part is very hot.
2. When we see the ''man in the moon,'' we are looking at mountains and _____ on the moon.
3. As far as we know, there is no food, water, or _____ on the moon.
4. The sun shines on half the _____ at a time.
5. The twelve _____ who have walked on the moon have taken away some of its wonder.

Write T if the sentence is True and F if it is False.

6. _____ In 1969, two American men were the first people to land on the moon.
7. _____ The moon gives off its own light.
8. _____ The sun shines on only half of the moon at any one time.
9. _____ It takes the moon about one month to move around the earth.

Find the one correct answer.

(10.) _____ Another good name for this story is
   a. "Learning More about the Moon."
   b. "Heat and Cold on the Moon."
   c. "How We See a Half Moon."

Check on page 164

BA-13▬▬▬▬▬**NO ONE LIVES FOREVER**

Write <u>T</u> if the sentence is True, <u>F</u> if it is False, and <u>?</u> if the story doesn't tell.

1. _____ Ellen knew the men in the car.
2. _____ The Harding place was 10 miles from Ellen's house.
3. _____ Ellen sang a song about dying.
4. _____ The man in the car wanted Ellen to help him.
5. _____ Ellen loved her farm and her pond.
6. _____ The water in the pond kept Ellen from dying.
7. _____ Ellen took money from the man.
8. _____ Ellen looked like an 18 year old.
9. _____ The fish in the pond were hundreds of years old.
10. _____ Ellen could live forever without the water from the pond.

138

Find the correct ending for each sentence.

11. _____ The old man wanted
12. _____ Ellen told the man
13. _____ Ellen didn't want anyone
14. _____ Ellen kept telling people

a. to go away.
b. to drink from her pond.
c. to find the Harding place elsewhere.
d. to live forever.

Find the one correct answer.

15. _____ A good new name for this story could be
a. "The Fish Pond."
b. "A Cake of Poison."
c. "A Large, Shiny Car."

Check on page 165

BA-14 ═══════════════ CARLOS SPEAKS UP

Show the order in which these events happened in the story by writing 1, 2, 3, 4, 5, and 6.

1. _____ Carlos calls the OSHA.
2. _____ Changes are made, and working is safer.
3. _____ Carlos talks to his boss about safety at work.
4. _____ A man comes out to look over the shop.
5. _____ Carlos talks to the men at the machine shop.
6. _____ Carlos waits to see if things get better. They don't.

Write one of the words in the box to complete each sentence below. Use each word only once.

machines	brighter	Maria	Mr. Block	boss
	OSHA	shop	accidents	

Carlos was worried because there were so many
7._____ at his shop. He found out about
OSHA from 8._____, his 12-year-old girl.
She told him that he must talk to his 9._____
first. If no changes were made after that, then Carlos
should call the 10._____ people. He called,
and a man came to look at the 11._____. Soon
there were new 12._____ and a 13._____
place to work. The men were happier, and so was 14.
_____, the boss.

Find the one correct answer.

15. _____ This story is about how Carlos
   a. quit his job before his boss could fire him.
   b. did something to make his shop a safer place to
      work.
   c. told Maria to speak up for her rights.

Check on page 165

Here are some facts about the World Trade Center. Write the letter of the numeral that completes each sentence.

1. The buildings are _____ feet high.
2. There are _____ floors in each building.
3. It takes _____ seconds to get to the top.
4. _____ people work there.
5. _____ people are needed to clean.
6. _____ cars can be parked underground.
7. It took _____ years to finish.
8. The buildings cost _____ million dollars.

a. 58
b. 500
c. 1,350
d. 7
e. 2,000
f. 30,000
g. 110
h. 800

Write <u>T</u> if the sentence is True, and <u>F</u> if it is False.

9. _____ Looking south, you can see the parks in New York City.
10. _____ You can't hear the street noises at the top of the building.
11. _____ There are all kinds of stores and shops in the buildings.
12. _____ All the people love working there.
13. _____ The World Trade Center will not be up for more than two years.
14. _____ There are many ways to get to the World Trade Center.

Find the one correct answer.

15. _____ This story is about
   a. going up in a fast elevator.
   b. how to find a job in the World Trade Center.
   c. two very tall buildings and what they are like.

Check on page 165

BA-16 ■■■■■■■ A HOME FOR ANNA

Write T if the sentence is True, F if it is False, and ? if the story doesn't tell.

1. ___ Ms. Stanton told Janet to come see a little boy.
2. ___ Janet and Bob were driving in the fog.
3. ___ A woman stopped the car and asked for a lift.
4. ___ Janet was a teacher.
5. ___ Angela told Bob not to drive so fast.
6. ___ Bob dropped Angela off at the train station.
7. ___ Anna's mother died five months ago.
8. ___ Anna's father died when she was two years old.

Show the order in which these events happened in the story by writing 1, 2, 3, 4, 5, and 6.

9. ___ Angela told Bob not to take Route 27.
10. ___ Bob told Angela he would give her a lift.
11. ___ Janet got a call from Ms. Stanton.
12. ___ Anna showed Janet a picture of her mother.
13. ___ Ms. Stanton told Bob and Janet about the accident.

14. ___ Ms. Stanton told Janet that Anna's mother had died in a plane crash.

Find the one correct answer.

(15.) ___ This story is about how
   a. Angela dies in a plane crash.
   b. Angela saves the lives of Anna's new parents.
   c. Driving in fog can cause a very bad accident.

Check on page 165

BA-17 ━━━━━THEY DON'T MAKE THEM LIKE THAT ANYMORE

Write T if the sentence is True, F if it is False, and ? if the story doesn't tell.

1. _____ Maggie had just moved into the building.
2. _____ Maggie had no children.
3. _____ There were no children in her apartment building.
4. _____ Maggie was an older woman.
5. _____ Maggie thought her life would stop when the silver clock stopped.
6. _____ The silver clock was worth two hundred dollars.
7. _____ When her glasses broke, Maggie was afraid she wouldn't get out safely.
8. _____ Maggie saved a little baby.
9. _____ Maggie got back from the hospital the next day.

Show the order in which these events happened in the story by writing 1, 2, 3, 4, and 5.

10. _____ Maggie sees her silver clock and takes it along.

11. _____ Maggie takes the small basket down the stairs.

12. _____ She finds Tommy and looks for the stairway.

13. _____ Maggie wakes up and smells smoke.

14. _____ Her glasses fall off and break.

Find the one correct answer.

15. _____ This story is about how
   a. Maggie saves something which she believes is very important.
   b. fires start in apartment houses.
   c. Maggie's cat finds his way to safety.

Check on page 166

BA-18 ━━━━━━━━━━━━━━━━━ **FIRESTORM**

Check the things that were <u>alike</u> in both the Siberian firestorm <u>and</u> the atomic bomb that fell on Japan.

1. _____ There was a very loud noise.

2. _____ The land was covered with forests and ice.

3. _____ There was a fireball in the sky.

4. _____ The land was burned out.

5. _____ Whole cities were wiped out.

6. _____ It left splintered trees standing.

7. _____ The crash was caused by a shooting star from outer space.

8. _____ After the crash, plants began to grow much faster and more wildly than before.

9. _____ There was a giant hole in the ground.

10. _____ After the crash, animals were sick and covered with sores.

Write $\underline{T}$ if the sentence is True, $\underline{F}$ if it is False, and $\underline{?}$ if the story doesn't tell.

11. _____ Kulik found a giant hole left by the falling star.

12. _____ The firestorm in Siberia was really an atomic bomb.

13. _____ If the firestorm had hit some other place, many people could have been killed.

14. _____ Kulik found very few animals in the forests of Siberia.

Find the one correct answer.

15. _____ This story is about
a. a ball of fire that lit up the sky.
b. giant holes in the ground.
c. a strange happening in the forests of Siberia.

Check on page 166

Show the order in which these events happened in the story by writing 1, 2, 3, 4, and 5.

1. _____ Sara knows she has found the pictures she needs.

2. _____ Sara looks for the right picture.

3. _____ Sara wins the contest and some new friends.

4. _____ Sara sees the ad for the picture contest.

5. _____ An old woman asks Sara to come over and talk.

Write <u>T</u> if the sentence is True, <u>F</u> if it is False, and <u>?</u> if the story doesn't tell.

6. _____ Sara was happy being a housewife and mother.

7. _____ She took a photography course.

8. _____ She had entered many contests before.

9. _____ The old woman was sad about the way her life had changed.

Find the one correct answer.

10. _____ This story is about
   a. how Sara finds what she's looking for.
   b. old people who find it hard to be happy.
   c. what you can learn in a photography course.

Check on page 166

1. – 3. Write a check in front of 3 ways The Animal House cares for animals.

a. _____ takes away big animals which live in small apartments

b. _____ tries to find new homes for unwanted animals

c. _____ makes people clean up the sidewalks

d. _____ cares for sick or hurt animals

e. _____ finds lost animals

f. _____ stops people from leaving kittens out to die

4. – 8. Write a check in front of 5 things we know for sure about the storyteller.

a. _____ is a man

b. _____ wants to be a vet

c. _____ really loves animals

d. _____ is very tall

e. _____ gets angry at people who don't treat animals well

f. _____ has many pets at home

g. _____ likes the job

h. _____ doesn't like zoos

i. _____ likes running after monkeys

Write T if the sentence is True, and F if it is False.

9. _____ Things always go well in this job.

10. _____ It is important to like animals in this job.

11. _____ People sometimes keep strange animals in the city.

12. _____ Some people don't "fix" animals because they don't want to pay for it.
13. _____ There are always homes for puppies and kittens.
14. _____ Cats can climb down trees more easily than they climb up.

Find the one correct answer.

15. _____ This story is about
   a. keeping a pet in the city.
   b. the work of The Animal House and its workers.
   c. what to do with too many puppies and kittens.

Check on page 166

BA-21 ━━━━━━━━━━ **THE STONE GIANT**

Find all the correct answers.

1. Which is true of the stone giant?
   ___ a. He was an Onandaga Indian
   ___ b. George Hill had him put in the ground at Stub Newell's farm.
   ___ c. He was more than ten feet long.
   ___ d. He had pores.
   ___ e. P. T. Barnum bought him for $60,000.
   ___ f. He is now at the Farmer's Museum in Cooperstown, New York.

Find the correct ending for each sentence.

2. ___ The well diggers found   a. a real man.

3. ___ Stub asked people who   b. a very large piece
       wanted to see the giant   of stone.
       to pay

4. ___ Some people thought the   c. a man of stone.
       giant was

5. ___ In Iowa, George Hull had   d. fifty cents
       bought

Write T if the sentence is True and F if it is false.

6. ___ Stub Newell was out of town when the giant was
       found.

7. ___ Not more than 2,000 people a day came to see the
       giant.

8. ___ P. T. Barnum stopped showing the Cardiff Giant
       when George asked him to.

9. ___ People found the true story about the giant funny.

Find the one correct answer.

10. ___ Another good name for the story is
       a. "How to Make a Stone Man"
       b. "The Last Train to Cardiff"
       c. "Stub Newell's Giant Joke"

Check on page 167

Find the correct ending for each sentence.

1. _____ Running can be
2. _____ It is important to
3. _____ A runner should start by
4. _____ People of all ages
5. _____ What you wear on your feet

   a. check with a doctor.
   b. find running a good sport.
   c. should fit and feel right.
   d. good for your health.
   e. running only a short time.

Write T if the sentence is True, and F if it is False.

6. _____ In a short time, a runner's legs get stronger.
7. _____ Giving a runner a lift in a car is a big help.
8. _____ Running is never good for the heart.
9. _____ A beginner should start running slowly.

Find the one correct answer.

10. _____ This story is about
   a. running as a sport.
   b. how running can hurt your heart.
   c. how cars can help runners.

Check on page 167

Write T if the sentence is True, F if it is False, and ?
if the story doesn't tell.

1. _____ Gina spent a lot of money when she was working.

2. _____ Gina didn't have the money to pay the November rent.

3. _____ Gina went on a TV game show.

4. _____ Gina didn't know the names of any of the songs.

5. _____ Gina won one hundred $100 bills.

Show the order in which these events happened in the
story by writing 1, 2, 3, and 4.

6. _____ The MC says she is wrong.

7. _____ Gina can't find a singing job.

8. _____ Gina gets on the game show.

9. _____ Gina sings her song on TV.

Find the one correct answer.

10. _____ A good new name for this story could be
a. "Gina Becomes a Winner."
b. "TV Game Shows."
c. "Tune Times."

Check on page 167

Find the correct ending for each sentence.

1. _____ Don was driving
at night because

2. _____ The police shot at
Don because

3. _____ Don couldn't
walk because

4. _____ Adi had to get a
job because

5. _____ Adi could help
her people
because

a. Don could no
longer work.

b. she could make
others understand
Indian ways.

c. he wouldn't stop
his car.

d. the bullet was
stuck in his back.

e. he had to get a
medicine man.

Check all the things that this story is about.

6. _____ how white people must be helped to understand the ways of Indians

7. _____ how sick young children can get

8. _____ how an Indian woman breaks with the
ways of her people and goes to work

9. _____ how much money a person can get from
the government

10. _____ how Don gets along in his new life

Check on page 167

Find the correct answer for each question.

1. _____ How do you know that the town is not an important place?

2. _____ How do you know that there isn't much to do in this town?

3. _____ How do you know that not many strangers come to town?

a. All the boys go to meet the train.

b. The train comes in only once a week.

c. It was a big thing when the woman got off the train.

Write T if the sentence is True, F if it is False, and ? if the story doesn't tell.

4. _____ The strange woman was a good listener.

5. _____ She paid Steven well for carrying her bag.

6. _____ She didn't know where to find a room.

7. _____ Steven liked to talk about his father.

8. _____ The woman had never been to the town before.

9. _____ Steven often had lunch with the woman.

Find the one correct answer.

10. _____ This story is about
   a. trains that come only once a week.
   b. winters in a small town.
   c. how a visitor brightens Steven's winter.

Check on page 168

BA-26 ━━━━━**A STRANGER COMES TO TOWN , PART 2**

Write one of the words from the box to complete each sentence below.

changed	winter	down	worthless	fly

1. No one could remember a worse _____.
2. Some of the older people looked _____ when the woman walked by.
3. Steven wished he could take off and _____.
4. The people of the town had made the woman feel _____ when she was a girl.
5. The woman learned that she and the people in the town had _____.

Show the order in which these events happened in the story by writing 1, 2, 3, 4, and 5.

6. _____ The woman says that she is leaving.
7. _____ Steven thinks his father knows who the woman is.

8. _____ A new train called the "Rocket" comes to town.
9. _____ Steven's father asks him about the woman.
10. _____ Steven leaves his town.

Write T if the sentence is True and F if it is False.
11. _____ The woman tells Steven what trouble she was in.
12. _____ She tells him to get out of town, too.
13. _____ Most of the people in town treated the woman well.
14. _____ Steven talked with his father a lot about the woman.

Find the one correct answer.

15. _____ This story is about
   a. the train coming to town.
   b. how the strange woman got into trouble and had to leave town.
   c. Steven's finding that he must leave his town to grow up.

Check on page 168

Find the correct ending for each sentence.

1. _____	Eating many foods	a. are what our bodies don't need.
2. _____	Easy foods	b. go bad after too long on a shelf.
3. _____	Junk foods	c. doesn't mean we eat the right foods.
4. _____	Dated foods	d. tell if the food is still fresh.
5. _____	All foods	e. may cost more, but they save time.

Check all the things that are important to remember in buying food.

6. _____ Is the food fresh?

7. _____ Who owns the store?

8. _____ What is the cost?

9. _____ What does the label say?

10. _____ Does the store run ads?

11. _____ What is the cost of fresh foods and the cost of frozen?

12. _____ What size can be used?

13. _____ Who works at this store?

14. _____ When will the food be eaten?

Find the one correct answer.

15. _____ Another good name for the story is
a. "Buying Frozen Foods."
b. "How to Be a Smart Shopper."
c. "Junk Foods."

Check on page 168

BA-28 ━━━━━━━━━━━━━━━━━━━━━━━ A FABLE

In each blank, write the correct word from the box. Use each word only once.

able	sticks	together
tried	farmer	dying
tied	strong	fighting

There was a (1)_____ who had eleven sons who were always (2)_____ . The farmer wasn't (3)_____ to make them hear when he (4)_____ to stop them.

When the farmer was (5)_____ , he asked his sons to bring thin (6)_____ to him. Then he (7)_____ the sticks together and showed his sons that they would be (8)_____ if they would stick (9)_____ .

Find the one correct answer.

10. _____ This story is mainly about
    a. a family that had to learn to work and live together.
    b. how strong sticks are when they are tied together.
    c. a farmer and his cornfields.

Check on page 168

BA-29━━━━━LAST OF THE SMALL-TIME FISHERMEN

Find the correct ending for each sentence.

1. _____ Mallorca is   a. money.
2. _____ *Pescado fresco* is   b. an island.
3. _____ *Pesetas* are   c. fresh fish.

Who did each of these jobs? Write P for Pablo and M for Miguel.

4. _____ sells fish in the village.
5. _____ mends the nets.
6. _____ cleans the boat and drys the nets.

Read the two paragraphs. All the missing words are in the box. Write the correct word next to each number.

fish	back	main	eight
meat	Pablo	low	smaller

Pablo goes to the village carrying fish on his
(7)_____ . He gets there before (8)_____ o'clock and goes
to the (9)_____ street first. Then he goes to the
(10)_____ streets. If he has fish left over, he sells
it at a (11)_____ price.

The people don't eat as much (12)_____
today because they have enough money to buy more
(13)_____ . But (14)_____ and Miguel will go
on fishing.

Find the one correct answer.

15. _____ What is this story about?
   a. Pablo selling his fish
   b. The hard lives of two fishermen
   c. Life in Mallorca

Check on page 169

Show the order in which these events happened in the story by writing 1, 2, 3, 4, 5, and 6.

1. _____ The doctor says that Paula is bleeding inside.

2. _____ In her sleep, Paula pulls Ray out of the waters.

3. _____ There is a bad car accident.

4. _____ In a deep sleep, Paula sees that Ray is drowning.

5. _____ The doctors say Ray will live.

6. _____ Paula and Ray are brought to the hospital.

Write T if the sentence is True, F if it is False, and ? if the story doesn't tell.

7. _____ Paula had these strange things happen before.

8. _____ The doctors always thought Ray would live.

9. _____ Paula died after the crash.

Find the one correct answer.

10. _____ Another good name for this story would be
   a. "What Saved Ray?"
   b. "Paula Is Cut."
   c. "It's Useless, Paula."

Check on page 169

ANSWER KEY

BA-1	BA-2	BA-3	BA-4
1. Joe	1. 4	1. PT	1. 4
2. Sam	2. 2	2. PT	2. 2
3. Sam	3. 5	3. T	3. 1
4. Sam	4. 3	4. T	4. 5
5. Joe	5. 1	5. T	5. 3
6. 2	6. F	6. PT	6. T
7. 5	7. F	7. T	7. T
8. 1	8. T	8. PT	8. ?
9. 4	9. ?	9. b	9. F
10. 3	10. T	⑩ c	10. ?
11. b	11. ?		11. T
12. c	12. F		12. T
13. a	13. F		13. F
14. b	14. T		14. F
⑮ a	⑮ a		⑮ a

BA-5	BA-6	BA-7	BA-8
1. b	1. e	1. Mr. Homes	1. 56
2. c	2. a	2. Ray	2. loved
3. d	3. b	3. Ray	3. think
4. a	4. d	4. Cloudy	4. good
5. 3	5. c	Day	5. F
6. 1	6. T	5. Angela	6. T
7. 5	7. ?	6. Ray	7. T
8. 2	8. F	7. Ray	8. T
9. 4	9. F	8. Angela	9. F
(10.) c	10. T	9. 3	10. F
	11. T	10. 1	11. T
	12. F	11. 5	12. F
	13. ?	12. 4	13. T
	14. ?	13. 2	14. F
	(15.) a	14. b	(15.) a
		(15.) c	

BA-9	BA-10	BA-11	BA-12
1. d	1. run	1. d	1. sun
2. a	2. got	2. f	2. craters
3. b	3. chicken	3. e	3. life
4. c	4. back	4. a	4. earth
5. 3	5. man	5. b	5. Americans
6. 5	6. winner	6. c	6. T
7. 1	7. d	7. T	7. F
8. 4	8. c	8. F	8. T
9. 2	9. b	9. F	9. T
10. c	10. a	10. F	10. a
		11. T	
		12. ?	
		13. ?	
		14. T	
		15. a	

BA-13	BA-14	BA-15	BA-16
1. F	1. 4	1. c	1. F
2. F	2. 6	2. g	2. T
3. T	3. 2	3. a	3. T
4. T	4. 5	4. f	4. ?
5. T	5. 1	5. b	5. F
6. T	6. 3	6. e	6. F
7. F	7. accidents	7. d	7. T
8. ?	8. Maria	8. h	8. ?
9. ?	9. boss	9. F	9. 3
10. F	10. OSHA	10. T	10. 2
11. d	11. shop	11. T	11. 1
12. a	12. machines	12. F	12. 6
13. b	13. brighter	13. F	13. 4
14. c	14. Mr. Block	14. T	14. 5
⑮ a	⑮ b	⑮ c	⑮ b

BA-17	BA-18	BA-19	BA-20
1. F	1. ✔	1. 4	1. – 3.
2. F	2. __	2. 2	a. __
3. F	3. ✔	3. 5	b. ✔
4. T	4. ✔	4. 1	c. __
5. T	5. __	5. 3	d. ✔
6. ?	6. ✔	6. F	e. ✔
7. T	7. __	7. T	f. __
8. F	8. ✔	8. ?	4. – 8.
9. ?	9. __	9. T	a. __
10. 2	10. ✔	(10.) a	b. ✔
11. 5	11. F		c. ✔
12. 4	12. ?		d. __
13. 1	13. T		e. ✔
14. 3	14. T		f. __
(15.) a	(15.) c		g. ✔
			h. ✔
			i. __
			9. F
			10. T
			11. T
			12. T
			13. F
			14. F
			(15.) b

BA-21	BA-22	BA-23	BA-24
1. b, c, d, f	1. d	1. ?	1. e
2. c	2. a	2. T	2. c
3. d	3. e	3. T	3. d
4. a	4. b	4. F	4. a
5. b	5. c	5. T	5. b
6. T	6. T	6. 3	6. ✔
7. F	7. F	7. 1	7. ___
8. F	8. F	8. 2	8. ✔
9. T	9. T	9. 4	9. ___
10. c	10. a	10. a	10. ✔

BA-25	**BA-26**	**BA-27**	**BA-28**
1. b	1. winter	1. c	1. farmer
2. a	2. down	2. e	2. fighting
3. c	3. fly	3. a	3. able
4. T	4. worthless	4. d	4. tried
5. F	5. changed	5. b	5. dying
6. F	6. 3	6. ✔	6. sticks
7. ?	7. 2	7. ___	7. tied
8. ?	8. 4	8. ✔	8. strong
9. T	9. 1	9. ✔	9. together
⑩ c	10. 5	10. ___	⑩ a
	11. F	11. ✔	
	12. F	12. ✔	
	13. T	13. ___	
	14. F	14. ✔	
	⑮ c	⑮ b	

BA-29

1. b
2. c
3. a
4. P
5. M
6. M
7. back
8. eight
9. main
10. smaller
11. low
12. fish
13. meat
14. Pablo
15. b

BA-30

1. 3
2. 5
3. 1
4. 4
5. 6
6. 2
7. ?
8. F
9. F
10. a